Green Meadow Girl

Green Meadow Girl

A MEMOIR

Ernestine McMillan Hilton

PastPerfect Publishing
Philadelphia PA
Austin TX

GREEN MEADOW GIRL

Copyright © 2011 by Ernestine McMillan Hilton

For information address PastPerfect Publishing
6601 Cuesta Trail, Austin, TX 78730.

ISBN: 978-0-9838925-0-2 (paperback)
ISBN: 978-0-9838925-1-9 (hardcover)
ISBN: 978-0-9838925-2-6 (ebook)

This book is dedicated, in loving memory to my two Earls. First, to my husband, Earl Lavern Hilton, my Incredible Man. He was a quiet man who, day by day, made his corner of the world a better place. We were married for 68 amazing years. Our adventures took us all over the world but we always returned to the Rocky Pine Ranch, our one true home. My Incredible Man passed away in October 2009.

Secondly, I dedicate this book to my other Earl, Earl Laverne Hilton Jr. From the time he was born we called him Sunny. His timely birth in 1944 almost certainly saved his daddy's life. In a time when his father was away fighting in WWII, Sunny gave me a reason to hope for a better world. Earl Junior died unexpectedly in December 1981 and took a piece of my heart with him. I think of him constantly and wonder what astonishing things he might have done had his life not been cut short.

Earl Lavern Hilton

Earl Lavern Hilton Jr.

Table of Contents

Acknowledgments

A SINCERE THANK YOU

To Mary, who polished my little stories into a readable book. To Rick, who kept me believing that this was a story worth telling. To Nancy and Jerry who gathered all sorts of material, took me around to all the old places, shaking me and humoring me into getting it all done. To Alison, who took wonderful photos of those old places, where memories re-surfaced and gave reality to the telling. To my brothers, Don and Ted, who helped me remember our growing up years. Thank you all for your wonderful support.

Cover photos: Background of Rocky Pine Ranch Meadow by Nancy Hilton 2011, front photo by Earl Hilton 1938. Cover design by Mary Parr.

Introduction

Prompted by the readers of my book, *Once Upon a Green Meadow*, I have written a sequel. Although it is not in every sense a true sequel, its pages bring back memories of those frugal years during the Great Depression when I was growing up. Having made it through the rugged childhood years, I was determined to forge ahead as best I could. Hard times robbed us of many things, yet I was resolved to follow the path I set for myself.

My teenage years were a time of great turmoil. The poverty endured by the people of America forced many changes in our society and the structure of our lives. Just as Father found that horses no longer pulled the plow and had to learn a new way of doing things, I too faced many challenges. While these changes were taking place, a great war descended upon us. I came of age on this stage of change and insecurity.

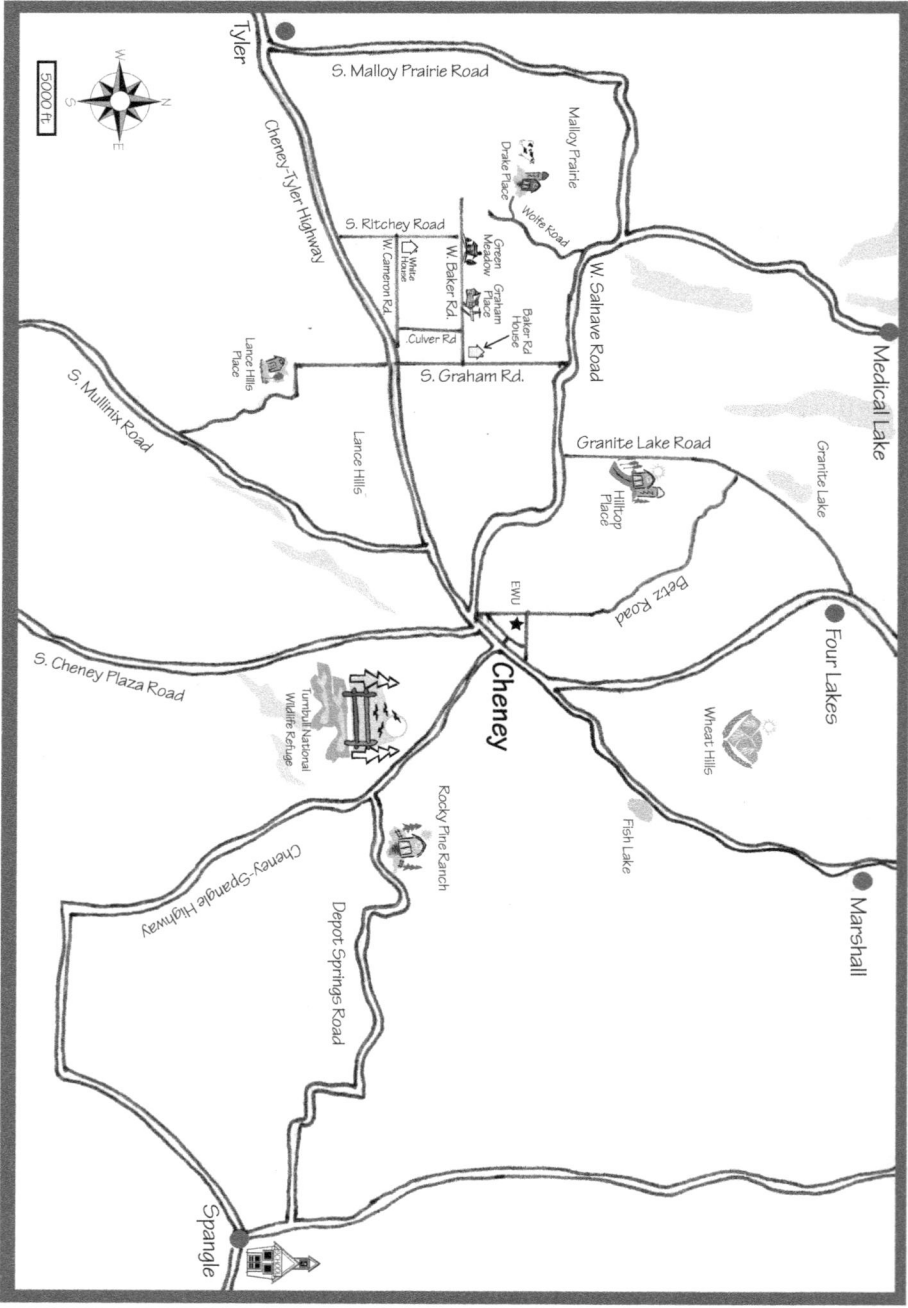

Goodbye to the Green Meadow

It is a hot afternoon in late summer. My sister Edith and I have come down to the little creek to say a last farewell to our home on the Green Meadow. We sit on a mossy hummock in the shade of an aspen tree, just below the big spring, and take off our shoes. Carefully, our toes test the cold water. Then we step slowly down into the creek. We know this may be our last chance to visit the creek that gurgles and sings on its way to the river and the far-away ocean.

Wading slowly along, we wiggle our toes in the creek's muddy bottom. We see a few frogs sleeping on lily pads, half-hidden under the big stalks of wild parsnip that grow along the banks. We slip by carefully so as not to disturb them. We are on our way to look at a house standing in a clump of trees almost a mile away. Because we have no money and no home, Father says that we are going to live in a new place.

Mother calls the house a little bungalow. From our home on the Green Meadow we can see it, far down the road, at the edge of a grove of trees. The house stares back at us with vacant eyes. The outside of it is painted a brilliant white. Everyone in the neighborhood calls it the "White House."

Since we must leave the Green Meadow, Father says it is sensible to move into this nearby vacant house. No one has ever lived in it. Our old neighbors, Cecil and Jack Long sold their ranch and moved away to work on the Grand Coulee Dam. Lots of families have gone away to find work at the dam. Perhaps the family that built this house went there too.

Edith and I are now opposite the house. We step out of the creek, put on our shoes and crawl through the fence. We follow the overgrown driveway up to the abandoned structure. From the outside it has the makings of a fine house. But, there is no front porch or stairs. The front door is so high off the ground that we can't reach it.

We wait, and soon Mother and the boys arrive, pulling their wagon loaded with big blocks of wood. These are the chopping blocks Father uses when he splits wood for the stove. Mother has brought them from the woodshed at the Green Meadow. She nails boards on the top of the blocks to make steps so we can go into the house.

We scramble up and push open the unlocked door. Nothing is finished. The walls are plastered but never painted. The floors are hardwood that has never been polished or waxed. But the living and dining rooms are spacious. There are three bedrooms with walls of unpainted boards.

There are no doors on any of the rooms inside the house. Mother sets to work hanging blankets over the bedroom doorways to give us some privacy. There are no closets for our clothes. One room looks like it was intended to be a bathroom, but has no plumbing. It seems that all the work on the house just suddenly stopped. The kitchen is too small to accommodate our breakfast table. Mother says we will eat at the big table in the dining room.

During the good years, as Father's herd of cattle grew, he had an arrangement to graze them on the White House's four hundred acres. I don't know what arrangements Father made now regarding the house. It has been vacant for a long time.

It is hard to think about all we are leaving behind. Our farm is gone forever, lost in the hardscrabble times folks call the Great Depression. The bank foreclosed on the mortgage because Father could no longer pay. All the cattle went to auction, and we have to leave our Green Meadow home.

Money is scarce. Father is searching for ways to make money to provide the things our family needs. There are plenty of tall pines on the new place, so Father has arranged to cut wood on shares. Father says well cut and seasoned wood is a good commodity these days. Everybody has wood-burning stoves for heating their houses and cooking meals.

Although it is moving day, Father is not here. He is up at Graham's Place helping with the haying. It's up to Mother and us kids to move our meager belongings down this dusty road. Earlier we sorted and packed up our things. Our beds were torn apart. Now the mattresses and springs are placed across the boys' red wagon. It takes four trips down Ritchey Road to complete the move. We all help Mother pull the little wagon.

Teddy is 7, Don is 9, Edith is 11, and I am 13. I don't believe that my brothers and sister really understand what is happening to us. Mother is sad, and we all try to cheer her up as we work.

The long moving day is almost over. We are hungry and tired. Finally Father comes home. Mother scrambles eggs, and we have fresh bread and butter. After supper, Father reassembles the beds, and we all fall into them and sleep.

The next morning Mother builds a rough shelter for her hens out under the trees. When all else fails, the eggs are our only source of cash. With Father away working for other farmers, she is left with so much to do on her own; the cattle, the milking, the chickens, the gardening and four young children. Mother calls it her helter-skelter time.

We are scarcely settled in this new place, when Father finds a job in the wheat fields of Ritzville, fifty miles away. Father has to care for forty horses. Every morning they have to be fed and groomed and ready to pull the big combines in the fields. During the day, Father works on the combine as a sack-sewer. Busy as he is, he tries to come home every other weekend.

Don and Ted are young, but they try their best to help. Mother milks the two cows we still have. There isn't enough milk to ship to the dairy, so any milk we don't use at our table is separated and sent to the creamery in Cheney. This is a time consuming chore. Frequent thunderstorms frighten us. With Father away we fear the fires that smoke and crackle in the forests not far from our home.

Father writes to us often, but there is no mail route on Ritchey Road. So we all take turns riding my horse, Trixie, the only saddle horse spared from the auction, all the way to our mailbox on Baker Road, hoping to find a letter there. Mother and Father have never been separated, and it is hard for them. Mother misses Father dreadfully and needs his advice on this new farm.

As summer comes to an end, I feel my childhood slip away. Leaving the Green Meadow and struggling to start a new home has seen to that. I cast my mind forward to September and my excitement about going to junior high school. I am 13, a teenager at last. Mother has made me a new dress. I even have new shoes. I have thrown away my old polio brace and high top shoes. My thoughts are all on the future.

The Journey to a New School

A crisp September breeze brushed our faces as we rushed out of the house, crossed the gravel road, squeezed under the wire fence and found the trail that would lead us through the woods to Uncle Ed's house. Then we began to run. Edith was in the lead. The boys and I were right behind her.

We ran hard, knowing that there was barely time for us to catch the yellow bus. We pounded up the old cow trail, dodged the tangle of low elderberry bushes and scratchy wild roses racing up the trail that was worn deep in the soil from years of cattle passing by. Dust flew from our flying feet.

When we arrived at Culver Road we barely had time to wipe the dust from our shoes and straighten our skirts and jackets, just as the yellow bus poked its nose up over the hill from Joe Graham's place. This was a special day. Not only was it the first day of school, it was the first day for me in the big junior high school in Cheney. As I settled down in my seat my thoughts raced toward the day ahead.

The bus stopped at Grier School just long enough for my friend Margaret, my sister Edith and my two little brothers to hop off the bus with the other elementary school students. Watching them leave the bus, I felt a twinge of regret, realizing that I was leaving behind the country school and the classmates I had grown up with. I was eager for what lay ahead. Cheney Junior High School was only five miles up the road.

When the bus pulled up in front of the school in town, there was an odd ache in the pit of my stomach. There was a moment of loneliness when I realized that I would know only a few students in this new school. Yet I was eager to take the next step. I knew I was ready to begin a new adventure.

Only one Grier School classmate came with me to junior high that morning. As the bus left us at the front door, Glen dashed ahead and ran into the schoolhouse, then down the stairs and into the gym. His buddies from the football team waited. He had been coming to join them for football practice for nearly two weeks now. I envied him for that.

It didn't seem right that my cousin Edna wasn't coming with me to the new school. We had always done things together. I missed her very much. She was still confined in the Edgecliff Sanatorium recovering from tuberculosis. It was up to me to make it on my own in the new school.

I stood back and let the other students in the bus rush out ahead of me. Then I stepped out and went up the big front steps, tugged open the heavy door, and walked slowly down the wide hall. The soles of my new shoes squeaked on the shiny floor. It felt like I was the only person in the building. I went down the long hallway until I came to the seventh grade classroom.

I peeked into the room. Empty. I was the first to arrive. I walked in, my eyes scanned the big room. It was almost as big as all of my old school put together. I counted the rows of seats. Ten down and five across. That was five times the number of students at Grier. Awed by the sheer numbers, I could not imagine that many kids all in one room.

Walking up and down the rows, I selected a seat, second from the front on the far side of the room, against a row of windows that looked out onto the street and the city park beyond. I settled into my seat, placed my tablet and pencil and my lunch sack on the desktop and took a long look around the room. The clean smell of the newly waxed desks and floor hung in the air.

I felt the warmth of the big room wrap around me. Any apprehension about the new school was swept away in the quiet classroom. I knew I was ready. I looked out at the park across the street. The beautiful old trees were showing the colors of fall. Looking beyond the park, I could see the campus of the State Normal School through the trees. There was my goal. I was now just one block away from the college. From childhood I had dreamed of going there to become a teacher.

When the college was founded it had been called the Benjamin P. Cheney Academy. It had been renamed the State Normal School two years later. In 1937, as it grew into the state's premier teachers college, the legislature decided to give it a new important name and it became Eastern Washington College of Education. The college would undergo two more name changes until it arrived at its final name, Eastern Washington University.

My years at the small country school had given me confidence. I was ready to continue my education at the bigger school. Over the years I had looked forward to attending the three-story junior high that sat up on the hill. I admitted to myself that I felt a pinch of apprehension when I walked into the big school. Then I remembered that Mother always said just be ourselves and things would work out all right. That thought, and my determination to succeed, settled me down inside.

I had known only a small number of friends at that point in my life. There were the children I had known from nearby farms, a few cousins and my small class from the Grier School. I knew I would see a few of those old chums here at Cheney Junior High. I didn't have long to wait. I was overjoyed to see my childhood friend, Clare, come through the door. I was pleased when she chose the seat next to me.

I recognized the next person who came in too. I had known Kenny McCall and his family from the many times I had gone to their place with my father. Father hauled wood from our farm to fill the McCall woodshed, knowing that they were a fatherless family. He felt it was his duty to make sure they had plenty of wood to keep them warm throughout the winter. I hadn't thought about Kenny being in seventh grade too.

I watched as Elizabeth came through the door, accompanied by several girls. She had been at Grier for a short time. Her family now lived in Cheney. Her father farmed the wheat hills off the Salnave Road. She smiled as she and her friends chose seats near the front of the room. Most of the students had been together since first grade. Only a few of us were newcomers. Yet somehow I felt welcome here.

Soon the big classroom was filled with boys and girls, and it was only a few minutes later that the bell rang and Miss Cecil Dryden, our seventh grade homeroom teacher, stepped into the classroom. She was a stately lady who wore her blond hair pulled back in a bun. She stood tall and poised in her slim tan skirt and crisp blouse. I liked her right away. When she spoke, she was calm and her voice was soft and kind.

The junior high school was staffed with professors from the college. Mother had told me that Miss Dryden was a published author of a book about local history. I felt in awe of her and waited eagerly to hear what she had to tell us. She was here to guide us through seventh grade English and inspire us to express ourselves on paper. Miss Dryden was so interesting that the morning flew by.

During our first break, Clare and I walked the halls of the three-story building, hoping to learn our way around in the big school. Finding a friendly janitor leaning on his broom, we asked him the way to the library.

"Just right on down the hall to the big room on your right," he told us.

The sight of the big room filled with books was such a delight that I went right to the desk and asked how I could check out a book. I knew that any time I could spare, I would spend in the library with my nose in a book. This big library was so different from the cupboards on the back wall in the Grier School room. I could hardly wait to take an armful of books home from those beckoning shelves.

Many thoughts ran through my mind that day. My confidence had grown over the years since I first set foot in the little one room school house. I had learned a great many things at Grier School. I missed the old friends I had left behind. Although I sometimes felt timid, I tried to act confident. Here at the new school I knew I would have to reach out to make new friends.

Cheney Junior High School
Photograph courtesy of the Cheney Historical Museum

Cheney Normal School
Later called Eastern Washington College of Education and
Eastern Washington University

WoHeLo

One afternoon as the school day ended, I saw Elizabeth's mother, waiting at the door.

"Would you like to come with Elizabeth and me," said Mrs. Mickey. "I want to take you to meet the Camp Fire Girls after school."

"What are Camp Fire Girls?" I asked. I had never heard of this before.

"It's a club for girls your age. We go on hikes in the woods. Sometimes we build campfires and roast marshmallows, like we're doing today," Mrs. Mickey told me. " I think you'll like it."

"We have lots of fun, "Elizabeth said. "Phyllis will be there and Lois and Clare."

"Clare will be at the campfire?" I asked. "She's never told me about it."

"She is going to join today," Mrs. Mickey replied. "Her mother is going to bring her. Come on, Elizabeth and I would like you to join us. I'll drive you home when the meeting is over."

That was enough to intrigue me, so off we went to Fish Lake, just a mile or so out of Cheney. Getting out of the car, we hiked into the nearby woods known as Shepherd's Canyon, and walked up a path beside a gurgling creek. Soon we came upon the group of girls, busily laying branches for a fire.

Clare was there with her mother, as well as the Camp Fire Guardian, Mrs. Lulu Cutting, and her daughter Marjorie. They called us over to sit by the fire that was beginning to crackle and flame. There were other girls from my seventh grade class seated around the fire. I had never been in a group of girls all the same age before. I had only played with three or four girls at a time, and then they were older ones and young ones.

We toasted wieners and marshmallows on sticks and sang songs. I learned to sing the Camp Fire song, "WoHeLo", that meant "work, health and love." There was another meeting next week when we would take a hike farther up the canyon into the woods to watch birds and learn their calls. I already knew many birds, and I was eager to learn more. I went home that night knowing that I wanted to be a Camp Fire Girl. It would cost $1, but Mrs. Mickey told me that she had already paid my membership.

I could hardly wait for next week to come around. Growing up on the Green Meadow had given me an intimate knowledge of the country that was admired by my new city friends. I especially enjoyed camping out in the woods. I loved the hikes, the campfires, and most of all, the companionship of girls my own age.

Camp Fire filled a real need in me. I missed being with my sister and our friend Margaret. I recalled our adventures in the woods picking flowers, or riding our stick horses, and playing in Little Creek, chasing polliwogs and bullfrogs. I missed my cousin Edna too. Mother and I had a talk about it, and she said it was just a phase in my growing up. She said that soon I would find other friends and different things to do. As always, Mother was right. I had found a very special group of girls who enjoyed the same things that I did.

Lulu Cutting, the leader of our group, was a local matron who proved to be the perfect mentor for girls my age. A dedicated member of the "social set" in our little town, she took her role as Camp Fire Guardian very seriously. Under her tutelage we grew and blossomed. She was genuinely interested in each of us, and coaxed and cajoled us on our way to adulthood. She became like a second mother to us all.

As our group leader she taught us the social graces as well as the practical side of housekeeping. She helped us give little parties where we brought together the interesting people in our community, from mill-workers to college professors. She taught us how to dress and how to walk and talk. As we grew older she taught us the politics of the town and introduced us to its leaders. She guided us in our choices and trained us to take an active role in our community.

Not only was she interested in teenagers, she cared about all people. She helped develop a center for senior citizens, the first in our town, with programs for elder members of the community to get out and about and take part in activities. She was dogged and determined, setting high standards for community service. She helped each of us find our own niche.

She often led us out to explore our little world. It was a world that was changing rapidly. The times in which we came of age would shape our lives in unimaginable ways. There were the difficult years of the Great Depression behind us and the trying days of World War II lay ahead. Without her patient guidance, many of us might not have recovered from the cruelties of what we had already suffered, or survived the difficulties that lay ahead.

THE LAW
OF THE
CAMP FIRE

Seek Beauty
Give Service
Pursue Knowledge
Be Trustworthy
Hold on to Health
Glorify Work
Be Happy

The Law of the Camp Fire from The Book of the Camp Fire Girls, 1929

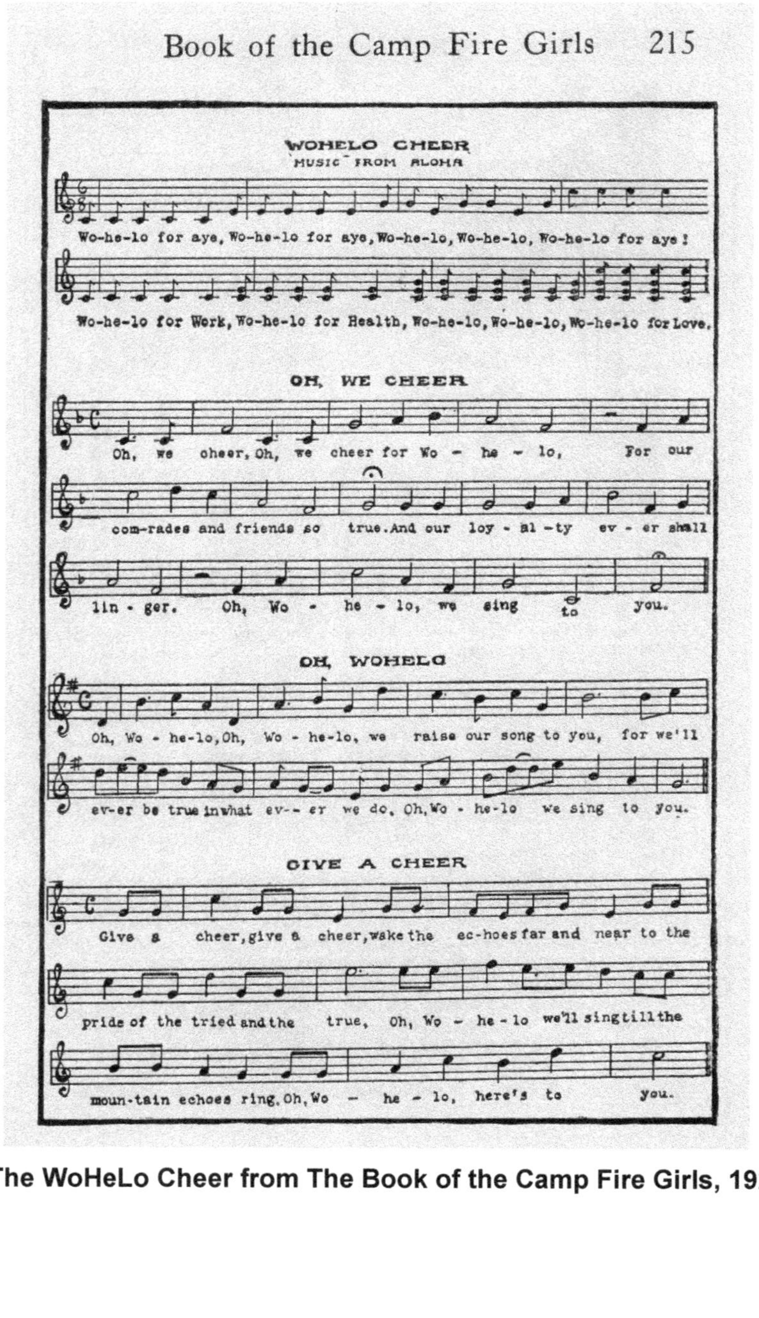

The WoHeLo Cheer from The Book of the Camp Fire Girls, 1929

The Move to the Graham Place

We spent a year in the strange white house on Ritchey Road. For me, it had been a joyful year. I was happy in junior high school in Cheney. I had made new friends and learned many new things.

But out on the farm, things were not going well. Most of the farm equipment and all of our cattle had been sold to pay off the mortgage at the bank. Father was left with very little to work with. All winter, Father spent long days out in the forest, cutting wood and selling it to customers in town. We survived the long cold winter in the white house. Now it was spring and another opportunity opened for us.

Our close neighbors, the Graham family, had also had a trying winter. Joe's brother, Virgil Graham had become quite ill. He had rheumatism and was unable to walk without crutches. With his grown daughter helping, they had managed to get through the winter. Now that spring had arrived, Virgil and his family were ready to give up their ranch and move into Cheney where they could live in relative comfort without so many chores. They were looking for someone to help with their ranch and the cattle they left behind.

One evening, Father said, "Remember how the Graham family stood by us through our trying times? We will always be very grateful for their help. I have been thinking it over. Maybe there is a way to repay the Graham family by helping Virgil Graham during his illness."

"That's a good idea," Mother said, coming out of the kitchen dusting the

15

flour from her hands. "But how can we help them? We don't have any money to give them. A few chickens wouldn't go very far."

Father explained further. "I think we could help them with their ranch. We could live in their house and milk the cows and take care of their animals. That would give Virgil some time to get well and time to decide if they want to sell the ranch. It's hard to make decisions when you don't feel good. If Virgil feels better in the spring, and wants to come back to the ranch, it will still be there."

"But how would we do that?" Mother asked. "What would we live on?"

Father spoke again, and we all listened carefully. "I've been thinking. We're not comfortable here. I'm sure their house would be much warmer than this one. Their barn and milk house are certainly much better. We could stay until they make up their minds about selling the farm. We could put up the hay this summer, keep everything warm in winter. We could live in their house and milk and care for their cows. We could divide the milk check between us."

Then I piped up. "Us kids wouldn't have to walk all the way up to Uncle Ed's to catch the bus. The bus goes right by the Graham place."

And turning to Father, I asked, "Could we really do that? It would be swell to just walk down the lane to get on the bus. Almost like living on Baker Road again!"

At that point, everyone got into the discussion, and before long we all agreed with Father that we should give his plan a try. The next day Mother and Father went to visit the Graham family, and Father made his proposal. The Grahams had been worried about finding someone to care for their ranch until Virgil got better. Virgil's brother Joe Graham and his son Norm had been taking care of the chores. But they had chores at home, and when winter came this would be hard for them. Virgil was thinking of putting an ad in the Cheney Free Press to find some help.

The Grahams liked the idea of having Father take care of their place, and they accepted the plan gratefully. The next weekend we went up to look the place over. Situated on Graham Road, the ranch adjoined the land where we had lived on Baker Road. We were already familiar with the

Graham place. We had roamed over its fields and played in its creeks and meadows. It reminded us of home.

The house was built in the late 1800s when the Graham family first came to the Graham Flats area. The rooms were large and could easily accommodate our family. There were three rooms upstairs, making it possible for Cousin Wally to come stay with us and continue his studies at the college.

Mother especially liked the kitchen arrangement. There was a regular kitchen, with a range, and plenty of room for our round oak table. Adjoining this kitchen was another kitchen. Called the summer kitchen, it was a large room, its sides open to the outdoors, and the roof was covered with creeping vines that shaded it from the summer heat. There was a range and sink where you could cook or do the canning outdoors. There was a downstairs bedroom and a comfortable living room with plenty of room for our piano.

The Graham family liked the smaller place they found below the railroad tracks in Cheney. It suited them just fine. They came one day and dug up some of their favorite plants to take to their new home, said a fond goodbye to their cattle, and were driven away by their daughter.

By this time, we were pretty good at moving. We put our belongings into the hay wagon, and pulled by the horses Bud and Molly, we made it to the Graham Place in one trip. Now we were living in a nice house again. Mother was glad to have a telephone. Wally came to stay in the extra room upstairs and helped Father with all the chores around the farm.

Earl and the Violin

With the move to the Graham Place, life began to get better for all of us. That fall, we no longer had to make the long walk to the bus stop. We only had to be ready and waiting. Wally had been hired as the school bus driver so when he drove off in the bus every morning, we were on it.

One morning I came to school early, and as I walked down the hall I heard music. I stopped to listen. Was that the school orchestra? I had never heard a live orchestra. I had only heard music played at local dances and records played on a phonograph. I was mesmerized by the sound.

As I went closer to the door, the music stopped, and I could hear the members putting down their instruments, preparing to leave the room. The teacher saw me and came to meet me. He asked if I liked music and if I played an instrument. I said I had taken piano lessons and could read music. I told him I had learned to play the violin by ear and played in a little band with some friends.

"I would like to learn to play the violin in the orchestra," I told him.

He said that all the chairs were taken in the violin section. There was no place for me. "However," leaning down toward me and smiling, he said, "there is an opening. Would you like to play the bass viol?"

The bass viol? What is that? I had never seen one. But if I could learn to play it, I would be playing in a real live orchestra. "Maybe," I replied, trying to sound confident.

18

Earl and the Violin 19

"Let's give it a try," he said, and I followed him to the back of the room. There a huge bass viol leaned in the corner. The teacher stood the big instrument up and held it. It was higher than my head.

"We'll get something for you to stand on, "he said. "It's like your violin, just bigger. You will stand beside it with your fingers on the strings, and play with the bow." He took the bow and pulled it across the strings. The big deep voice vibrated through the empty room.

All I could think of was the sound of the orchestra that I had heard as I came down the hall. I decided that I would try to play the bass viol. At least I would be playing in the orchestra.

On Monday, Wednesday, and Friday mornings, before school started, I went to the orchestra room to practice the viol. The first days were brutal. I learned to put my fingers on the fat strings and pull the bow across. I was trying to learn the music, knowing when to chime in with that deep fiddle sound. My years of piano lessons told me it was possible. But I could tell that it would not be easy.

One morning when I was practicing the "Big Brute," as I secretly called it, I looked up and there stood a tall good-looking boy smiling at me. He held a delicate violin in his big hand. Our eyes met, and we stood looking at each other. I saw that he was nicely dressed. His tan corduroy pants had a crisp crease. A soft blue sweater covered a pressed white shirt. His dark brown hair was perfectly combed.

We stood there for a moment, just looking into each other's eyes. Then we began to talk. He told me that he had joined the orchestra hoping to play the saxophone. Instead he had been given a violin. I sensed right away that he was not very happy with the fiddle. When I told him I wanted to play the violin in the orchestra, he laughed and said, "here, you can have mine."

I shook my head, and we both laughed. He told me his name was Earl Hilton and from that moment on we became friends. After that we both came early to practice. We laughed and teased each other. I found out how much he loved music. He knew all the popular songs.

Soon he was writing little notes made of song titles and slipping them into my hand when we left the room. Playing the big bass in the orchestra was not all that great, but the little notes Earl wrote did something to my heart. Here is one of them:

*Dear **Beautiful Brown Eyes,***

You Do Something to Me. Them There Eyes** are just a **Cheerful Little Earful. Any Time's The Time To Fall For You.

Earl

Earl was a city boy who came from Seattle to a ranch in the meadowlands of East Cheney Township when he was 10 years old. He was good at math and loved music. He and his parents got along well together and never missed a musical movie, often going to Spokane to attend the Sunday matinees.

His easy relationship with his folks carried over into his friendships, including me. He never seemed judgmental, accepting everyone just the way they were, but living up to his own principals.

Earl liked sports, but didn't go out for them like other boys, feeling that he was needed at home at chore time. He enjoyed the competition on the judging team in his classes in agriculture. This led him to become a member of the Future Farmers of America. He admired his teacher and coach, Wren Pierson, and worked hard to win blue ribbons in stock judging contests with other schools.

Earl liked track and baseball. On warm days during the noon hour, he played baseball. I would watch from the second floor window. He would step up to the plate, look up at me, then hit the ball so hard it would fly over into the park across the street. He would look back up at me and grin, then go on with the game, pretending I wasn't there.

One day, during the noon hour, I was in the library looking for a book when a girlfriend rushed in and told me, "You better go out the west door. Earl and Ralph are going to have a fight over you."

"A fight? Over me?" I didn't believe anything like that could be happening. I ran down the stairs and into a classroom where I could look out the window and see what was going on.

I could see a crowd of boys milling around at the foot of the steps. They were yelling, "Fight! Fight!" and were jumping around.

Then I heard somebody say, "Ralph is going to knock Hilton's block off for dancing with his girl."

His girl? What girl was he talking about? I wasn't Ralph's girl. One Saturday evening, when I was playing for the dance at Harmony Schoolhouse, I had danced once with each of them. I knew I wasn't Ralph's girl, and I wasn't sure if I was Earl's girl either. Worried, I decided to hang around and see what would happen.

Just then I saw Earl come out of the schoolhouse. I held my breath. The boys milling around on the sidewalk surged forward to the foot of the steps yelling, "Fight! Fight!"

I was watching Earl. He paused and stood quietly looking down from the top step at the guys on the sidewalk below. He said not a word, but stood silently on the steps.

The chant began again, "Hit him! Hit him! He says you been fooling around with his girl."

For another moment Earl stood there, then he moved quietly down the steps. One of the fellows at the foot of the steps moved forward to stop him. "Hey," he shouted at Earl, "what are you going to do?"

Then the whole bunch shouted "Yeah! What are you going to do? Come on, fight him!"

Earl paused, his head up. He looked them over quietly, then he said, "I am going to go downtown and get my mom a loaf of bread." And he stepped down onto the sidewalk and headed downtown.

No one moved. Ralph quit jumping around and just stood there, his mouth open, watching Earl walk down the sidewalk toward town. No one said a word. They just turned around and went into the schoolhouse, leaving Ralph standing there all by himself. I let out a long sigh. I guess I might be somebody's girl after all.

As we grew, our relationship grew. I looked up to Earl. He was always neatly dressed, quiet and polite. Unlike many other couples, we did not seek shadowy corners to hang out in. He had his classes and his stock judging friends. I had my work on the school newspaper and the Camp Fire Girls.

Earl & Ernestine
Our first picture. I wore my pink dress. My cousin Wally tool the picture.

The Potato Roast

Before we moved to the Graham Place, Father had hurt his back while cutting wood during the long cold winter. He had also suffered a cold that had settled in his chest and left him with a bad cough. With all the worry Father faced along with the humiliation of losing the farm and the herd that he had so carefully bred, his health had been declining.

On the Graham Place with Wally to help with the chores, Father began to improve. He found time to prune some of the trees and brush around the buildings. He made a pile of the debris out on the edge of a little meadow below the house.

One October day, we all went out to dig the potatoes and put them away in the cellar. Father always grew fine Netted Gem potatoes, with a dusky netted brown skin that were perfectly formed for baking. They were always sweet and delicious even without butter. We all admired the potatoes as we put them away.

"Why don't we invite the neighbor kids over and have an old fashioned potato roast? We could burn the big brush pile, and after it has burned down, we can bake the potatoes in the ashes," Father suggested.

"That would be a great way to get together with our old neighbors," Mother said, clapping her hands. "I could phone around, and you kids could invite a school friend or two. Wouldn't that be fun?"

We hadn't had much fun lately, and that sounded like a great idea. Soon

Mother was on the phone, inviting the neighbors. Mother said that Edith and I could each invite a favorite friend. Edith chose her new friend, Lucille Billesbach, whom she admired so much because she too had beautiful red hair. I knew whom I wanted to invite. But first I thought I should ask my mother. When she came to kiss me goodnight, I asked her.

"Would it be all right if I invited Earl Hilton to our potato roast?"

"I think that would be a splendid idea," Mother replied. "We could all get to meet him."

The next morning at school, I felt a little shy and almost afraid to ask Earl. I liked him very much, but I didn't know if he would like to come to my house. When we came out of the orchestra room at school, I slipped a little invitation to him. The next day when we met in the hall, he told me that he would like to come to the party.

"I'll come out on your bus, and Dad will come and get me after the milking is done," he told me.

That hadn't been so hard after all. Then I began to think and worry. Do I really want him to ride out on our bus? Where will he sit? What if the kids tease us?

"You know you have to have a pass to ride on a bus." I told him.

"Sure." He said, "I have it right here." He fished it out of his shirt pocket and showed me where his mother had signed it.

I couldn't help but be impressed. But I still worried. What would I do if he wanted to sit with me? What if the kids, or Wally, teased him?

The afternoon of the party, Earl hung around with a bunch of kids, and when our bus came, he got in line and walked to the back of the bus and sat down where all the big kids sat. I heard somebody ask him where he was going.

He said quite calmly, "I'm going to the McMillan potato roast."

Most the other kids said they were coming too. So that settled that. I learned right then not to worry about that Hilton guy.

Earl always seemed to know what he was doing. Although he liked to tease, he was always friendly and never quarreled with others, feeling that everyone was entitled to their own opinion. Most of all, I found that he was quiet and polite, easy to talk to, and a gentle person who would never hurt anyone.

The party turned out fine. Mother had added hot dogs to the menu, and we all had a fun time. While the potatoes roasted in the bonfire, we played games and chased each other around in the dark, finally settling down beside the fire, talking and telling stories. After the milking, Father, Mother, Wally and several of the neighbors came and sat around the dying fire with us, eating hot dogs and potatoes. It was great fun.

After his milking was done, Earl's dad came to get him and shook hands with Mother and Father. When everyone had gone home, the fire was thoroughly doused and we were getting ready for bed, I asked Mother how she liked Earl.

"He's quite a handsome young man," she said. "And very polite. You will be lucky if somebody doesn't try to snatch him away from you."

Earl Hilton

Earl & Ernestine

Taffy Pulls and Sleepovers

Edith and I enjoyed popular music, but we could no longer afford piano lessons. Such luxuries vanished when we lost our home on the Green Meadow. But we still had our piano. Mother called it our status symbol. Sheet music cost only ten cents, and we often copied or shared music with our friends. In the winter when Wally stayed with us, he added his banjo to our musical evenings.

Fun came back into our lives on the Graham Place. Edith and I learned to play popular songs on the piano, like *Blue Hawaii* and *Paper Moon*. We could ask a friend to stay all night. Mother would make divinity candy, and we had taffy pulls. Kids from school would beg to come.

Mother was happy. She sang at her work and wanted to dance again. She begged Father to get permission from the school district to have community dances in the old school house. It was just down the road, where Salnave and Graham Roads came together. She phoned some of the neighbors, and the ladies came down and cleaned up the old school building.

Saturday night we had a community dance. There was an old organ there that Mother could play. Kimbal De Young, who lived in the big house on Baker Road where we used to live, played clarinet. I played my fiddle and mother played cords on the organ. The neighbors came, and everybody danced. That was how my dance band began.

The helter-skelter time of the white house days were behind us. For the first time in a long time, we heard Father whistling while he worked.

We were back in our old neighborhood with friends close by. Edith and I were in our teens now, going to school in town and finding many new things to do.

Mother made wonderful candy. She made fudge, taffy and popcorn balls, but divinity candy was her specialty. She was known all over the neighborhood for her wonderful confections. Our friends at school liked to come to our taffy pulls.

Mother's taffy was a simple recipe of molasses, sugar, butter and vinegar. The concoction was mixed with water and heated on the woodstove until it bubbled. She would test it occasionally by dropping a spoonful into a cup of cold water. When Mother judged it to be the perfect temperature, the hard ball stage, the hot liquid taffy was poured onto buttered plates to cool. As soon as the candy was cool enough to handle, it was cut into smaller portions for pulling. Kids paired off as partners. If they tried to handle it too soon, there would be blistered fingers.

Taffy pulling was usually accompanied by peals of laughter as we pulled the warm gooey candy over and over. It was stretched out and then roped back together until it became a light honey color and satiny in texture. The pairs tried to think of fancy ways to fashion their candy to look the best. Sometimes they would pull it out into thin ribbons and braid it.

When the candy began to cool it wouldn't stretch any more. If you misjudged your timing you would end up with an ugly lump, still edible, but not very pretty. The trick was to cut it into bite size pieces at just the right time with buttered scissors. A taffy pull afternoon passed quickly and our friends took home a jelly jar full of delicious candy to share with their families.

We soon found that our city friends loved to come to the country. We were allowed to invite friends to stay overnight with us. Usually this would be on a Friday night, so we could stay up late. Edith and I shared an upstairs bedroom, with a big bed that could hold three girls. We also had a little cot in our room, so the one who had the friend sleeping over got to sleep in the big bed and the other took the cot. We often started out the evening altogether in the big bed because it was more fun. But when we got tired of the pranks and the stories and ready to settle down, one of us would slip out of bed to sleep on the cot.

Having girlfriends overnight was a great treat. Chores could be put off for a few hours while we slept in on Saturday morning. But eventually the work had to be done. The city girls especially liked helping with collecting eggs and feeding the chickens or working in the vegetable garden. The tasks that Edith and I dreaded, they thought were fun.

Edith and her girlfriend, Lucille, loved to analyze their dreams over breakfast. Mother would fix a special breakfast for us as we lingered at the table, long after the rest of the family had gone to their chores. They sat with their auburn heads bent close together breathlessly recounting dream adventures that always seemed to include good-looking boys from school. Naturally, they were the very same boys the girls were interested in dating. I think their dreams were mostly fiction because I doubted that even the most active minds could have so many adventures in only one short night of dreaming.

Sometimes I had girlfriends come for sleepovers too. Home life had become easier. With Wally living with us, our chores were easy. Wally had taken on the heavy tasks and was a great help to Father. Once again our family sat at the table in the evenings after supper, reading and playing cards together.

Edith's Big Summer

When school was out that summer, shy little red-headed Edith entered a contest at the Cheney Free Press. The person who solicited the most subscriptions to the paper, would win a brand new bicycle. We had lost our ponies in the foreclosure auction and we went about mostly on foot. How great it would be if Edith could win a bicycle, but it seemed like an impossible task.

Every day she got up early and walked around the neighborhood, talking to everyone, persuading them to buy a subscription to the Cheney Free Press. She called up old neighbors and family friends. She walked miles up and down the roads, knocking on doors, explaining how very much she needed that bicycle. At night she would fall into bed exhausted, but she would be up early in the morning, at it again. We admired her determination and were so proud of her. We all cheered her on.

The contest ended the night before the fourth of July. We all waited anxiously for the results. Time seemed to stand still. Then the phone rang. Father answered with his usual quiet greeting and listened carefully to the voice on the other end of the line. He hung up and we all stared, holding our collective breath. Then Father smiled his slow smile. Edith had sold the most subscriptions. Edith had won the bicycle! We cheered and clapped her on the back. Our very own Edith had won.

The next day was Saturday, the special day that Edith would be awarded the bicycle. We all dressed in our best, piled into our car and Father drove us to town. Edith stood on the sidewalk, beside the owner of the Cheney

Free Press while a crowd gathered, and she was given the shiny new bicycle. She was so proud. None of us had ever won a contest before. And certainly no one in our family had ever owned such a shiny new machine. The bicycle was a thing of beauty.

Edith didn't want to try riding it in front of all those people, so she pushed it up the sidewalk to our car, where Father helped her put it in the back seat. It was exciting to watch all the townspeople cheering on the sidewalk as we drove away.

Father decreed that this bicycle belonged to Edith, and to her alone. It was hers to ride and take care of and do with as she wished. None of the rest of us could ride it unless she gave her express permission. She practiced riding around and around in the big gravel yard at the Graham Place. It wasn't long before she had mastered it well enough that Father said she could ride it up Graham Road to Salnave Road, to show it off to her friend, Doris Jean.

All that summer, Edith rode around on the new bicycle. She generously allowed the rest of us to try out the two-wheeler. But we had to be very careful, and jump off quickly and keep a good hold on the bike so we didn't smash it up. We were all in awe of it, and we didn't take any chances of denting it.

Just before school was to start, Edith rode her bike all the way into Cheney to show it off to her friends. She told us how wonderful and free she felt, pumping hard up and over the hills of Salnave Road, the wind in her face and the hum of the tires on the blacktop. She came back home on the Cheney-Tyler Highway, where the road was paved, and there weren't so many hills. It was a great adventure. Riding her shiny new bike, knowing how hard she had worked for it, gave her a new confidence that she had never had before.

Bicycle Ad 1934

Ernestine and Edith

Independence Day

We spent only one year on the Virgil Graham Place. By the following summer, Virgil Graham's health had improved. He liked living in town and made up his mind to give up the farm. He placed the land and cattle up for sale, and we had to find another place to live.

A man my father knew, who lived in Deer Park, owned a farm on Wolfe Road. His name was Mr. Drake. The farm was just off Salnave Road, a few miles from Medical Lake. It was situated on the edge of a pine forest down a dirt road that ran along the back side of our old home on the Green Meadow. His land extended out onto Malloy Prairie, where he grew large fields of hay to feed his herd of dairy cows.

He advertised for a farmer to work the land on shares. Father applied for the job, and we soon moved away from Graham Road and went to live on the Drake Place. This posed some problems for our family. The new place was in the Medical Lake school district.

I was in Cheney Junior High and wanted to continue school there. I loved my school and had many friends. My sister Edith was starting junior high, and Don and Ted would soon follow. We all wanted to go to school in Cheney. The problem was how to get there from the new farm. There was no school bus on the Salnave Road. It was up to us to find our own transportation.

Father had saved enough money while working on the Graham Place to buy a nice used car. It was a 1932 Chevy, dark green with roll-up windows. Father declared that I was old enough to learn to drive. Then I could drive us all to school in the fall.

All summer I practiced driving our new car. In the evening after chores, Father would go with me as I drove up and down the country roads. It didn't take long to master the car and soon I thought I was ready to get my driver's license. Learning to drive was pretty straightforward. Studying the rules in the Driver's Manual was not so bad.

However, before I could get my license, Father decreed that I must learn to change a tire. He felt that I should know how, in case I had a flat out on the road. Blowouts were a common occurrence. A tire consisted of an inflatable inner tube inside a rubber tire. They failed frequently, especially on rough country roads.

Thus began my tribulation. Changing a tire was an ordeal of monumental proportions. Every evening after supper, I practiced jacking up the car, taking off the tire, getting the inner tube out and gluing a patch on it. Then I had to put it all back together. The big tire iron I used to pry the tire off the wheel took all the strength I could muster.

I struggled with the jack and I sweated as I twisted the lug bolts off the car. I had to take the inner tube out of the tire, pretend to fix an imaginary hole in the tube, then test it in the watering trough to make sure that it didn't have any bubbles. Then, I had to wrestle the inner tube back into the tire and put the tire back on the car, all under the watchful eye of my father. I fought the tire with grim determination, working until my muscles quivered with exhaustion.

Then Father would say, "You're going to have to do better than that, Sis, or you'll be stranded out there on the road somewhere all night." I kept at it. Finally, one evening late in the summer, Father came into the house and said, "Get your hat, Sis. Let's go get your driver's license." Father had judged me ready to drive.

We got in the car, and I drove over the wheat hills on the Salnave Road into Cheney. Captain Florence Morgan, Chief of the State Patrol, lived on G Street, just above the Shell station on 2nd Street. Father knew everyone in town, including Captain Morgan. We often saw him at the service station when we bought our gas.

Captain Morgan was an imposing man, a towering giant in a State Patrol uniform. Serious and very dignified, he always spoke to Father and tipped his hat. I was quite in awe of him. The idea that I would have to speak to him was enough to make me shiver. But I wanted my license.

I knew I had to drive if I was going to stay in Cheney Junior High. So I went quietly up the steps like a martyr to the scaffold. Captain Morgan shook hands with us and welcomed us in. The Captain and I sat at the kitchen table and he asked the questions from the booklet, *Rules of the Road*. I answered every question perfectly. I had memorized the book.

When the inquisition was over, Captain Morgan said, "now let's take a drive."

I got into the driver's seat silently. I was so scared that I was trembling. I tried to pretend that it was Father sitting beside me. I drove down 2nd Street, then up the hill to the college and back down again. Up and down and around town, as Captain Morgan gave the orders. Behind the wheel, I became more confident, and after awhile we drove back to his house. Then he signed my brand new driver's license, shook my hand and said I had done just fine.

On the first day of school, I got behind the wheel and drove myself and my brothers and sister to school. The boys hopped out at Grier School. Then I drove on into Cheney with Edith beside me in the front seat. I was 14 years old and I had won my independence.

The Power of the Press

My first two years of junior high school had passed quickly. My third and last year of school proved to be even more exciting. Our homeroom teacher that year was a young man in his thirties named Hank Beuchel. He was also a member of the college faculty as a history and economics professor. He served as our history teacher and also coached boys' football and basketball.

I remember him as a handsome and friendly teacher. Everyone liked him and the boys he coached looked up to him. Our class had been introduced to a smidgen of Washington State history the previous year under Miss Dryden. Now this teacher introduced us to a new subject called Social Studies.

We were living in an exciting time in our country's history. Mr. Beuchel brought the world right into the classroom. Soon we were immersed in current events. Franklin D. Roosevelt was president. His reelection campaign was an exciting race, and political enthusiasm was high. Our young teacher was anxious to bring us face to face with American politics, and we were eager to listen and learn.

We had lived through the crash of 1929 and the long, hard years of the depression. We had first-hand experiences that tumbled us right into the debates as to how our nation was being governed. The problems of the nation were not only on the front page of the newspaper, they were in our homes and in our community. Under the tutelage of this inspiring teacher, we ninth graders plunged into political discourse like seasoned voters. We took sides on every issue and debated with passion.

I recalled the summer afternoons when, as a child, I had hidden behind my grandfather's rocker while my father and uncles discussed the issues of the day. Now here I was, learning in class and pondering issues much as I had under that old chair. I understood how important it was that citizens be active and informed. I wished that I was 21 so I could vote.

Our ninth grade class was responsible for a little weekly paper about school events that was mimeographed and handed out to students. I dreamed of becoming its editor. Somewhat timidly, I approached the teacher with this suggestion. At first he shook his head. Then as I continued to argue, he gave in and told me that I could begin by helping him select the items to appear in the paper, and to write an editorial. I accepted the opportunity gratefully.

Things went along fine for the first few issues. Then I succumbed to temptation and made a critical error. Living through those desperate years of the Great Depression, I was very excited about the ideas Roosevelt was proposing to turn the country around. I was fascinated by all the ways the government was trying to bring prosperity back to the people. Inspired by all of this, I wrote a rousing editorial for the school paper. It was all about Roosevelt's New Deal. How proud I felt when I saw my words in print.

My euphoria didn't last long. The little paper was handed out on Friday and the students took it home with them. Monday morning when we arrived back at school, we found heated discussions taking place. I couldn't understand where all the excitement was coming from, or exactly what had brought on such wild happenings.

Apparently some members of the community had become upset over the editorial I had written in the school paper. Someone had complained to the school board. Members of the Board had taken sides. It had spilled out into the community. Over the weekend the town was embroiled in a hot debate.

One member of the school board had seen the editorial and immediately demanded that Professor Beuchel be summarily dismissed. He was appalled that a teacher had allowed such blatant political propaganda to appear in the school newspaper. On the other hand, the only woman on the Board had taken the opposite side. She insisted that it was good for students to be interested in politics and have opinions.

Monday morning she and the other board member had confronted each other on Main Street in front of the post office. Their argument became so heated that folks stopped to listen. The excitement ended when the man slipped on the snowy pavement and fell into the gutter. Almost immediately, the story was all over town about how the lady had knocked the man down.

My teacher told me about the consequences of my editorial, but did not scold me, nor suggest that I was wrong to have written it. He assured me that I had the right to express my opinion, even as a student, and made it clear that he was responsible for what appeared in school publication. The school principal was present during our talk.

I was stunned at the thought that my little editorial was causing such a big uproar. As always when trouble arose, I felt a desperate need to talk with my father. But we had no telephone and there was not enough time to get home. Noon hour came and I decided to go downtown and talk to some of our old friends, the shopkeepers who had known me since I was a child.

I signed out and walked downhill to Main Street, my mind in a muddle. The first business I came to was the drugstore. The pharmacist had known me since I was a small child. I knew he was a respected member of the community and had been a friend of my parents over the years. When I timidly admitted my concern about my editorial in the school paper, he assured me that it would all blow over, that I was not to worry. While we were talking, our family doctor, whose office was above the pharmacy, came in and joined our conversation. He laughed about the uproar over such a innocent story and told me not to worry about it. He thought the town needed a little excitement and that it would soon be forgotten.

I went back to school, still feeling troubled by the incident. Newspapers had always been an important part of my life. My earliest memories were of being held on my father's lap as he read me the funnies. The newspaper was the source of news in our home. But now, I had learned the power of the press. I couldn't help but be intrigued by the consequences of my editorial. It was from then on that I became really interested in writing. The responsibility of putting thoughts into words that expressed an opinion was electrifying.

Fishing for a Kiss

When I was a freshman in high school, Earl and I began our official courtship. On a fine Spring day in April, he invited me to go along on a fishing trip with his parents. They were going to Williams Lake about thirteen miles southwest of Cheney. Earl's parents were avid fishermen and were always anxious for fishing season to begin. As soon as the weather turned warm, they were getting out the fishing gear and making plans. Williams Lake was great for trout fishing.

I was surprised when Father agreed that I could go. He had always been afraid of the water and never allowed his children to try swimming. My family didn't take vacations, and even if we did, I'm sure my father would never consider going anywhere near water. I was secretly pleased that he trusted Earl to keep me safe.

The four of us walked down the dock and got into a little rowboat. I had never been fishing before and had hardly any idea what to expect. I sat quietly while Earl and his parents concentrated on baiting their hooks and getting them into the water. I loved being out on the lake in the rowboat. The weather was warm and a fresh breeze blew across the water. There didn't seem to be a whole lot to fishing. It was mostly sitting quietly and waiting. These were two things that I was already very good at.

After Earl and his parents caught several fine rainbow trout and put them in a bucket, we rowed back to shore for a picnic. After lunch, Earl suggested that we go out in the boat alone. We got into the boat and Earl rowed it out across the water with long sure strokes. I admired the way he handled the boat, like he had done it many times before. His parents weren't the least bit worried about him taking the boat out alone.

We rowed for quite a while. Earl steered out past a little peninsula and around a bend. We were out of sight of his parents. He pulled the oars into the boat and came over to sit next to me on the seat of the rowboat. Then he gently put his arm around my shoulders and pulled me toward him. It was then that Earl kissed me for the very first time. We spoke very little as we rowed back to the picnic spot where his mom and dad lounged in the afternoon sun. There was a new unspoken agreement between us and we had sealed it with kiss.

Ernestine and Earl at Williams Lake

Toward the end of that school year, Wally began planning a trip to Plummer, Idaho to visit his parents and celebrate his sister Edna's homecoming. Edna was coming home from the tuberculosis sanatorium. I was delighted to be invited along. It had been so long since I had seen my cousin. When I visited her at the sanatorium, I had to stand outside her window and we shouted back and forth. That could hardly even be considered visiting. I was so excited that we could be together and even touch if we wanted to after two long years.

Aunt Mamie's family was living in a small rustic cabin in the woods. The garden bloomed with white syringa and lilacs, their sweet perfume and the lazy hum of bees filled the air. Edna came skipping down the garden path to meet us. The two of us had a long hug.

Edna and I had to stand back and take a good look at each other. We had not seen each other up close for two years. We had both changed so much. Edna, who was a year and a half older than me, had grown into a beautiful young woman. I too had grown and was no longer the skinny little kid I used to be. We hugged and giggled.

Cousin Edna Flock

The June day was perfect. The sky was brilliant blue with a few wispy clouds scudding by on the breeze. The picnic took place in the yard, with Edna's brothers and sisters crowded around. Edna looked beautiful. Her cheeks were a rosy pink and she glowed with renewed health. Her mother pinned a pretty rose corsage on her shoulder.

After all the excitement of the picnic was over, Edna and I went up the rustic stairway to her room in the rafters of the cabin. There was so much to talk about that we both began to talk at once as we tried to make up for the lost years. Edna begged to hear all about my new beau, Earl Hilton. I told her about our first kiss on the lake. It was such a sweet romantic secret. I couldn't imagine sharing it with anyone else in the world but Edna.

The next day Wally drove us home. On the way he stopped to pick up his girlfriend. Then we stopped and got Earl at Rocky Pine Ranch. For the first time, Earl and I rode home in the rumble seat of Wally's car.

Blizzard, Fire and Flood

Mr. Drake had a large herd of cows to be milked. Don and Ted were barely old enough to help, but they spent long hours at the barn, helping with the milking. Mother milked too. Drake had installed a Delco System, a series of batteries that provided electricity to run the milking machines. This was the first time Father had used milking machines, so he had to learn how to operate them.

There was electricity to the house, but we were limited in how much we could use. We had electric lights, which we enjoyed, but they could only be used sparingly and turned off promptly when you left the room. If left on too long, they would use up all the electricity in the system, then everything would go dark. We had a radio for the first time, but we only listened to the noon news, and a fifteen-minute spy story, called *"Pretty Kitty Kelly"* that had caught Father's attention.

The only other electric appliance was an electric iron. This was something that Mother enjoyed very much, and we girls found ironing much easier, compared to the old flat irons that had to be heated on top of the stove.

Whenever the milking machines were working at the barn, we had to do without electricity at the house. After shutting everything off at the barn, there was about a half hour left in the batteries for us to use at the house in the evening. When that time was used up, the lights would go out, the radio would go dead, and we would be in the dark again. It took several hours for the batteries to recharge. It was essential that we have enough electricity in the batteries to power the milking machines in the morning.

Mother got a nice surprise when Dr. West's wife bought an electric washing machine. Knowing that our family faced many difficulties, the doctor gave Mother their old gasoline-powered one. Mother was delighted. Although the gas machine was noisy, it certainly turned out wonderfully clean clothes.

Mother washed everything in sight. Bedding was stripped from the beds, run through the washer and hung out to dry on the clothesline. Curtains were taken down and washed and ironed. Any clothing left lying around ended up in the washing machine. Although the motor clacked and clattered, and was a glutton for gasoline, it was a marvelous machine. It was Mother's first modern washing machine and she loved it. She threw her old washboard away.

Mother, Myrtle McMillan, at the Drake Place 1937

The year I was a sophomore in high school, we had a terrible winter. It snowed and snowed until all the roads were blocked with huge drifts. We couldn't find a way to get to school. Father tried with the horses, but the snow was too deep for them to pull a sled through the drifts.

Finally we ran out of supplies, and Father and Mother went in the sleigh with the team of horses, down through the trees to Tyler, to get food and other necessities for the house and barn. It was bitter cold and Father didn't want Mother to go, but she insisted that they could help each other if there was trouble.

For many weeks the Salnave Road was blocked with high drifts of heavy snow left by the storm. Many other roads in the area were also impassable. People had to find ways to get around the drifted areas. For weeks we had to take Graham Road out to the Cheney Tyler Highway, then up the highway to Grier School to drop off the boys, then on up the highway to Cheney.

All of this was costing us more gas and time to get to school. It was April before a big rotary plow, used by the railroads, finally came to clear away the snow. At last we were able to go up Salnave Road to school. With snow piled in the big cuts through the hills, the snow was higher than the car in many places.

That winter we had a fire at the house. It was early in the morning and barely light enough to see to get around. Father was awake and dressed and had started a fire in the fireplace. Suddenly there was a loud shout up the stairs.

"The house is on fire!" Father shouted.

Those were such dreadful words. We roused our brothers from their bed, and Edith and I threw all our clothes from our closet onto the mattress and the two of us, one at each end, managed to carry mattress and all down the stairs and out into the safety of the yard.

Creosote in the chimney had built up and caught on fire. We stood outside, shivering in the cold winter air, watching sparks fly up from the chimney top like Fourth of July sparklers. The fireplace was well built so only the creosote burned. The rest of the house was safe. However, we were all badly shaken. When the fire was out, we carried all our things back upstairs. We were so grateful that the fire had not been a bad one.

Spring arrived very late that year. Suddenly it was exceedingly warm. A Chinook wind was blowing out of the south. A Chinook is a warm dry wind blowing down the eastern slopes of the Cascades. Such a wind can make a foot of snow vanish in one day. The snow partly melts and partly evaporates in the dry wind. It was the worst possible thing to happen after a winter of such heavy snowfall.

The snow melted rapidly turning little brooks and streams into boiling rivers. Ponds and pothole lakes overflowed their banks. Water poured over the bare gravel roads washing out culverts and leaving ruts and holes. Roads became impassable again from the Spring runoff. We never knew when we started out for school, just what road we would find washed out or which road we should try.

One afternoon coming home from school, we found roaring torrents tearing out the bridges over the creek. Each road we tried was impossible. There seemed to be no way to get home. Finally we decided to go back to Baker Road and try going past Joe Graham's place to a little dirt road we knew that went to Bert Meyers place, then back onto the Salnave Road.

When we got to Graham's place, we found that the little ponds on either side of the road had overtopped their banks. The fast melting snow had covered the road. We pondered our dilemma. By this time, the sun was going down and we were afraid to be caught out at night not knowing which road was safe.

The four of us talked it over, and decided that, since Don and I had galoshes, we would wade up the road, measuring the depth of the water and try to locate any big potholes. Don reached out over the edge of the road and cut two long willow branches with his pocket knife. Then he went down one wheel track, and I went down the other. We took each step carefully, poking the sticks into the water ahead of us, testing the ground. This seemed to take forever, but we encountered no holes or washouts. We decided to chance it. I drove across slowly, everyone hanging on in case we lost a wheel in some marshy spot. Safely across, we headed home by way of Bert Meyer's place.

When we arrived home, we expected to find our parents sick with worry and overflowing with sympathy as we breathlessly recounted our harrowing adventure. However, Father was furious with me. He said it had been a foolish and dangerous thing to try. We might have broken off a wheel and been dumped, kids, car and all, into the pond. He said we should have gone around by Tyler even though it was miles out of the way.

Barn at the Drake Place
Photo by Alison Hilton, 2011

Teddy and the Bull

At the Drake Place we all struggled. It was one of the hardest times we ever faced as a family. The house was big enough, but we never had time to relax and enjoy it. We were cut off from our old neighborhood. We no longer saw our friends. We didn't have a telephone. The mailbox was a mile and a half out on the Salnave Road, but it didn't matter. Father had no time to read a paper and Mother seldom sat down to write a letter.

We worked from dawn to dark and still the chores piled up. We were dragging from exhaustion, never quite catching up. There were bitter arguments and acrimony between family members as each blamed the other for slacking. Even the land was sad. There was no meadowland with sweet grass where birds sang. There was no Limberlost with its dark mysteries. At the Drake Place on Malloy Prairie, the land was bleak and windswept. Tumbleweeds gathered at the fencerows.

Even we kids seemed to scarcely know each other anymore. Ted was in his last year at Grier school, Don was in junior high school. Edith and I were in high school. Every day was all about hurry. We hurried to school. We hurried home and hurried with our chores. There were no games and no more music. The piano was silent. Mother stopped singing and Father stopped whistling as he went about his chores. The joy had gone out of our lives. Mother and Father were so exhausted that when we needed help with our problems, there was no time to talk things over.

Mr. Drake did not deal fairly with Father. He often violated their agreement. Father was supposed to be paid a monthly salary and a share of the offspring of the cattle, but Mr. Drake took what he wanted, and was often slow in paying Father his monthly check. Although Father worked hard, he felt that he had to beg to get what was promised him. There was not enough money to pay the bills. Father was angry and troubled.

We children were faced with work beyond our years. There were forty cows to milk twice a day. The boys and Mother helped with the milking. Keeping the milk barn spotlessly clean was a daily chore. The barn had to be ready for inspection at any time so that the milk could go to market. Edith and I worked in the house as well, making meals and washing and hanging laundry.

One day the bull went missing from his pasture. Father sent 10 year-old Teddy out to find him and bring him back to the barn. It was nearly dark before Ted finally found the bull, off with some cows in a field halfway to Tyler. Ted tried his best to drive the bull back home, but the bull was determined to go the other way. It was getting quite dark, so Ted decided to leave the bull and come back to get him in the morning.

He started walking home. He kept walking and walking. Finally he came to a sign. It was so dark that he had to climb up the signpost to see what it said. The sign read 'Tyler'. Ted had been walking the wrong way. It was over 11 miles to Tyler. No wonder the bull refused to go that direction. The animal knew his way home. The little boy turned around and trudged homeward in the dark.

When the bull came back to the corral without Ted, Father was frantic with worry. What if Teddy had been hurt? Bulls could be dangerous. We all went down the road to find him. Father whistled and whistled and finally Ted answered in the dark. We all ran down the road to meet him. Poor little Teddy was worn out.

The Bull

The House with the Sad Face

I first saw the old place that came to be known as Rocky Pine Ranch when I was 8 years old. It was an August morning in the summer of 1928. My Grandfather McMillan had come to our farm on the Green Meadow to fetch Cousin Ona. He was taking her to his farm in the rolling hills near Mica Peak at the edge of the Palouse. Ona was going to help Grandmother during the wheat harvest. I was going along to keep watch over my 2 year-old twin cousins.

Grandpa brought us a box of sweet cherries from his orchard, and was taking back a big bundle of gunny sacks that Father had patched. The sacks would be filled with wheat harvested at Grandpa's farm.

We set off at first light in the little democrat wagon pulled by Grandpa's big grays, hoping to beat the heat of the day. We sat together up in the seat at the front of the wagon, with me squeezed in between Grandpa and Ona. When I got tired of the bouncing wagon, I could lie down on the pile of gunny sacks in the back of the wagon and watch the tree tops sway above us as we plodded along the dusty road.

This was the first time I would be away from my parents. I liked listening to the jingle of the harness and the clip-clop of the hooves on the country road. I liked going with Grandpa. He was an amiable traveler and always liked to explain things. When we got to Cheney and turned south, past the towering columns of the Martin Flour Mill, we bumped over the railroad tracks and onto the gravelly road to Spangle. As we passed the little railroad station, Grandpa pointed out the grove of tall poplar trees growing just below the tracks.

"There," he said, pointing to where several old poplars stood, their leaves rustling in the early morning breeze, "that is all that is left of the old artesian spring that gave the town its first name, Depot Springs. But then when Benjamin P. Cheney, who owned the railroad, gave a lot of money to build a school, the folks changed the town's name to Cheney in his honor."

Grandpa explained that Depot Springs Road had been important in the early days of the territory. The road was built to accommodate the farmers of the Palouse, who lived at the northern edge of the wheat-producing region and hauled their wheat to market in Cheney. Cheney had been the railroad hub for transporting wheat to market in those early times.

As we traveled on the way to Grandpa's house, we went out the Cheney-Spangle Road, bouncing over the rough gravel for three and a half miles until we came to Depot Springs Road. We turned onto the winding road as it wandered between rocky ledges, past green meadows through forests of tall pine trees. Thickets of wild rose bushes and chokecherry filled the roadside. We crossed a wooden bridge that spanned the creek that drains the meadows of Rocky Pine Ranch. The wagon rattled and shook. The horses snorted and tossed their heads as their hooves clopped over the bridge.

Although I had made many trips over that road with my family, I still remember that special ride with Grandpa in the wagon with his team of grays. The clop of the horses, the rhythm of the wagon as it bent back and forth over the bumpy road, and the happy voice of Grandpa singing an old hymn wrapped me in cozy contentment.

As we traveled along we came to a bend in the road where a very tall pine tree stood. Grandpa pulled the team and wagon off the road under the big tree for a better look. He pointed to the huge fork in the tree, several feet above the ground, where the tree's trunk separated into two smaller trunks that towered skyward. There at its fork was a level place, big enough for a person to curl up in.

"See that!" Grandpa exclaimed, pointing to the wide space where the two tree tops converged. "Wouldn't that make a wonderful bed, up there among those sweet-smelling pine needles. Someday I am going to bring my bedroll and climb up in that tree and take a snooze!" And he laughed his big jolly laugh as we looked up into the tree.

Picking up the reins and clucking to the horses, Grandpa drove the wagon around the bend and came out on a flat point of scabland overlooking a meadow and small pond where a few mud hens and ducks paddled about. I saw an old house all alone on a rocky knoll. The hill where it sat was sprinkled with bright pink bitterroot blossoms, but the old house looked sad. Its front porch sagged off to one side. The windows were broken and bricks had tumbled down from the chimney. It looked abandoned and forlorn.

"Looky there!" Grandpa said, shaking his head and pointing his finger up the lane. "There's the house with the sad face!" Grandpa clucked his tongue and snapped the reins. The horsed plodded on and I forgot all about the house with the sad face.

When I was 16, I found myself pulling into that same lane and visiting that house for the very first time. I had come down Depot Springs Road from the Beaughan place, just around the next bend in the road, where I had delivered a dozen fertile eggs to Mrs. Beaughan. She was hoping to hatch some white Leghorn chicks to add variety to her flock.

As I came back along the road I noticed the pond and realized that this was the farm where the Hilton family lived. Although I had known Earl Hilton for three years, I had never been to his home. He and his parents sometimes picked me up at my house to take me to the movies or a picnic, but I had never been to his place. I liked his Mother and Father and felt that I would be welcome, so I decided, on the spur of the moment, to stop for a visit.

It was a lovely May morning. I drove my father's car down the hill and pulled up at the back door of the old house at Rocky Pine Ranch. As I pulled up beside the house and shut off the motor, I was instantly surrounded by a dozen little faces, scampering over my car, bouncing up on the hood, peering in the windows, their eyes shining as they ran their tongues over the slippery surface of the windshield. Goats. Little kid goats.

Earl's father came out of the house laughing, and shooed the kids away. "Looking for Earl?" He asked. "He's down at the woodcutter's shack at the far end of the pond."

"Can I drive there?" I asked.

"Sure," he said. "If you're careful. Just stick to the upper edge, the meadow is a little swampy."

I drove down through the wire gate and out along the meadow, heading for the woodcutters shack that I could see in the distance. I hadn't gone a hundred yards when I hit a sodden spot and buried my car up to its hubcaps in mud. The car could go no farther. With a sickening burp of mud, my wheels sank even lower. What a disaster. Oh, the humiliation! There I was, casually dropping in on my best beau's family for the first time, and I found myself stuck in the mud.

I looked up toward the house where Earl's mother and father stood on the porch staring at me. Earl had seen the fracas and come up to meet me. I sat, red-faced, in the car afraid to get out for fear of sinking in the bog in my only pair of decent shoes.

The hired man came down from the barn with a team of horses and pulled my car out of the swamp. I was mortified to have caused so much trouble. Earl and his dad exchanged a look and I swear I saw an amused wink pass between them. I attempted to make a graceful exit by declaring that I would call again at a better time. However, Mr. and Mrs. Hilton insisted that I come in for a visit.

Stepping inside the house that my grandpa had always called the 'House with the Sad Face', I found it had a new life. Although the outside was much the same, inside it was very different. It was like a sophisticated city house. It was filled with comfortable furniture, nice drapes, and beautiful pictures on the walls. Inside, it bore no resemblance to its shabby exterior. Earl's mother had a fine touch and the old house gleamed under her hand. She was a friendly hostess and I soon forgot about my embarrassing entrance.

Rocky Pine Ranch House built in the late 1800s

Rocky Pine Ranch House, side view

Dating Earl

Cheney had its own movie house, the Melodian. With its two-toned stucco and Spanish style roof it stood near the intersection of Main and College Avenue. It was owned by Miss Lou Neilson. When it opened in the fall of 1929 even my father was persuaded to go. He laughed his head off at the silent Laurel and Hardy movie.

By the time I was in junior high school it was showing movies with sound and going to the pictures was all the rage. The first time I attended a movie with Earl was when our class was invited to an afternoon matinee. Earl slipped a note into my hand and asked me to sit with him. As I walked into the theater with some girlfriends I found Earl waiting near the door. As we entered the theater, rich red carpet runners were soft under foot. Bouquets of flowers in the foyer smelled sweet. The walls and ceiling were covered in Spanish leather. Spanish-style lights gave the theater a warm glow.

Earl told me that he had a favorite place to sit, on the left aisle, five rows down, "just right," he said, "to hear and see the movie."

We slid into leather seats, so cool and soft. I tipped back my head and looked at the ceiling, the ornamental plaster was beautiful. Tickets were 15 cents for children under 18, but that day it was free.

The movie was "*Captains Courageous.*" It was an adventure story about a spoiled little boy who fell off an ocean liner and was rescued by a fisherman. He became a member of the fishing boat crew and learned humility and love. When the hero, played by Spencer Tracy, fell overboard and drowned, I was in tears. Earl said not a word but passed me a nice white hanky. I wiped my eyes and tried to smile when I handed it back.

"Wow" he said, wiping his own eyes with the hanky, "What a great movie!" and he squeezed my hand and gave me a teary smile. He wasn't ashamed of a few tears himself. There in the dark we held hands. I think we fell in love that day at the movie.

Melodian Theater circa 1940
Photograph courtesy of the Cheney Historical Museum

By the time we were in high school we were hooked on movies. Although Earl had been going to the movies with his parents for years, they were new to me. I soon learned the names of all the actors and actresses. Earl liked musicals. Ginger Rogers and Fred Astaire were his favorites. He also enjoyed Charlie Chaplin, Laurel and Hardy and Buster Keaton, and we never missed a Mickey Rooney and Judy Garland picture. But most of all I loved sitting in the dark, holding hands, and watching the stories come alive on the screen.

Cousin Wally had a car with a rumble seat. He and his date would often take Earl and me to the movies with them. Wally was older and he made a fine chaperone. We rode in the rumble seat, with hair flying and the dust chasing us.

Melodian Theater in the 1930s
Theater is the building on the right with a star
Photograph courtesy of the Cheney Historical Museum

When we were teenagers, a date to the movies was a great thing. Although we were going to be sitting in the dark all evening watching the screen and barely looking at our dates, making ourselves gorgeous for the occasion was an important part of the fun. Edith and I would start dressing right after supper. We usually tried on dresses all afternoon, but that didn't mean we had made our final selection.

I would get so upset with my sister. She would try on all her clothes, reject them all, then she would start trying on my clothes. She would put something on, look at it in the mirror and decide she didn't like it. She would then just toss it on the bed. There it would be, all wrinkled, when I came to get ready and decide what I would wear. I would end up heating the iron on the stove and pressing my dress all over again.

Earl had to help his dad with the milking, so he never got over to pick me up until the first showing of the movie was well underway. The second movie usually started around eight o'clock and he liked just hanging around our house until it was almost time for the show. I used to tease him that he came to visit my brothers, not me. He liked talking with Don and Ted, and didn't mind how long it took me to get dressed. Sometimes we would barely make it to the last showing.

HANG ME UP

Melodian
Theatre
CHENEY

Programs Subject to Change Without Notice

BOX HOLDER
R. F. D.

Sec. 435½ P. L. & R.
U. S. POSTAGE

1c PAID
Cheney, Wash.
Permit No. 8

R. Evans, manager. Shows begin at 7 p.   Feature pictures begin at times stated below.
Adults 30c plus state tax 2c and Federal   3c—30c.   Children under 13 years, 10c

Hang me up and keep me lest you forget   a splendid programs we are showing this month.
Double Feature, or Single Feature, and Well Selected Short Subjects.

ALL SHOWS BEGIN AT 7:00 P. M.

News on All Sunday Changes

SUN. MON. TUES. AUG. 4-5-6
7:30-8:55 THE GHOST BREAKERS
With Bob Hope, Paulette Goddard
A mystery comedy of an heiress in
an allegedly haunted house.

Wed. Thurs. Fri. Sat., Aug. 7-8-9-10
7:10-8:55   NEW MOON
Jeanette McDonald, Nelson Eddy.
Romance and music the equal of
"Naughty Marrietta."

SUN. MON. TUES. AUG. 11-12-13
7:10-9:00   SUSAN AND GOD
Joan Crawford, Fredrick March.
Social comedy of a woman who tried
to run the world, but couldn't run
her own home.

WED., THURS., AUGUST 14-15
7:40-8:50 LONE WOLF MEETS LADY
Warren Williams, Jean Muir.
A dectective story.
Our Gang comedy 'Bubbling Trouble'

FRI. SATURDAY, AUG. 16-17
7:40-8:50   Henry Goes to Arizona
Frank Morgan, Virginia Weidler, Guy
Kibbee and Slim Summerville.
A comedy—Frank's troubles started
when he inherited a ranch.

SUN. MON. TUES. AUG. 18-19-20
Double Feature
7:10-8:20— PHANTOM RAIDERS
Walter Pidgeon, Florence Rice.
The breaking up of a Central Amer-
can sabotage and insurance racket.
8:20-9:25 GRANDPA GOES to TOWN
The Higgens Family.
A comedy with many difficult
situations, but all ends well.
9:25-11:00 "Phantom Raiders"

WED., THURS., AUGUST 21-22
7:40-8:50 JOE AND ETHEL TURP
CALL ON THE PRESIDENT
With Ann Sothern, Lewis Stone.
The mailman lost his job so the
Turps called on the president.
Cartoon, "Greyhound and the Rabbit"

FRI., SAT., AUGUST 23-24
7:35-8:45 LIGHT of WESTERN STAR
Victory Jory, Jo Ann Sayers and Noah
Beery, Jr. One of Zane Grey's best
known sagas of the West with magnificent outdoor photography.

SUN. MON. AUGUST 25-26
7:40-8:50   WOMEN IN WAR
Elsie Janis, Wendy Berrie, & Patric
Knowles. A story of the lives of nurses
behind the front line trenches.

Shows begin 7, features at times shown

TUES. WED. THURS. AUG. 27-28-29
Double Feature
7:00-8:10   IN OLD MISSOURI
Weaver Brothers and Elviry.
The story of sharecroppers changing
places with their landlords.
8:10-9:15 The CAPTAIN IS A LADY
A good comedy.
9:15-10:25 "In Old Missouri"

FRI. SAT. AUGUST 30-31
7:20-8:50   FLORAIN
Robert Young and Helen Gilbert.
A colorful and romantic story of
the collapse of the golden days of
Austria under the Hapsburg, featuring
a superbly intelligent horse whom all
animal lovers will enjoy.

Melodian Theater Program

Earl waiting for me on the porch

Edith dated often, and had a string of boyfriends. She would date one boy for a while, then get tired of him, and find somebody new. She liked playing the field, as she called it. She was perky and pretty and a wonderful dancer. She especially liked the jive and jitterbug. She enjoyed watching sports, mostly because she liked watching the boys on the field, and knew all the players at the games.

I, on the other hand, thought Earl was a fine date. He was easygoing and fun. We liked the same things and we liked each other. In high school, with my busy life, I didn't have much time for dating. But I did like boys. I enjoyed talking with them. They had much more interesting topics of conversations than girls did. But for dating, I liked reliable Earl. I didn't care to play the field. Earl and I started out with a fine friendship that over time grew into love.

When we were in high school, and there was a football game, Earl often took me downtown after the game. I would ride on the handlebars of his bike, and we would join our friends at the Malt Shop on College Avenue. All of this was totally new to me. I had never heard of a black and white sundae, a chocolate malt, or a banana split.

Once Earl got his own car, we liked driving around the countryside out over the wheat hills, singing along with the radio. We loved to sing together. Earl installed a radio in his car and he knew all the latest songs. Sometimes he would write me clever little notes, with song titles making up the message.

In August when Earl's birthday came around, his family had a big picnic down at Fish Lake. Earl loved the water, but I didn't know how to swim, so I enjoyed just lounging in the sun, watching him goofing around and showing off with his cousins.

We spent much of our time with each other's families where we enjoyed family gatherings, especially at holiday times. Earl was an only child, and he enjoyed boisterous times with my brothers. We liked to hike around the ranch and I often helped his mother with the evening chores.

A Day at the Chronicle

As I left junior high school and joined my classmates in the high school across the street, I knew what I wanted to do. The first class I signed up for was journalism. I wanted to learn all that I could about the newspaper. I admired the straight-forward way stories were told in the paper. So much was going on in the world, and I wanted to be part of telling it.

The year I was a junior in high school, an opportunity presented itself. The Spokane Daily Chronicle held a Newspaper Day. Schools from around the county were invited to send one student from each high school journalism class to spend a day at the newspaper. I was honored to be chosen as the student to represent Cheney High.

Fourteen of us gathered at the Chronicle office on a Friday morning. We were asked to choose how we wished to spend the day at the paper. I chose to sit beside the City Editor. My first task was to rewrite the stories that came in over the teletype machine. These stories came in from around the world. My job was to condense them into just a few words to fill up spaces in the paper. Although the job itself was a little dull, sitting beside the City Editor, Newland Reilly, gave me the chance to see how a big newspaper was put together. More importantly, I met the reporters as they checked in with the City Editor who assigned them their jobs.

That morning I met Rowland Bond when he checked in at the Editor's desk. Right away, Mr. Bond took me under his wing. All that day, when a news opportunity came up, he would interrupt me while I was at work at the rewrite desk.

"Want to come along, kid?" he would ask. "'So & So' is coming in on the 10:30 plane. Let's go meet him."

Out on the street, he hailed a cab and off we went. He took me with him to meet the several people who came into town that day. There weren't many planes coming into Spokane. The airport was out in the Valley at Felts Field. But Spokane was an up-and-coming city, and notable people were coming and going. Most of the people interviewed that day were there to take part in conventions, address a club, or attend a business meeting. I watched and listened as Mr. Bond greeted the newcomers. I paid attention to the kinds of questions he asked. I pulled out my notebook and pencil and mimicked Mr. Bond as he fired off questions and jotted down the responses.

I was just a kid soaking it all in. Mr. Bond took his guests to the best hotel in town, the Davenport. He made sure that they were comfortable and acquainted them with the city, so they would feel at home. Watching and listening to those interviews with a real reporter from a big city newspaper was a great experience. Although I didn't know at the time, Rowland Bond was one of the best in the business. Bond did the interviewing. I listened, learned, and wrote it down. We started the day strangers but we quickly became a good team. Bond was relaxed, friendly, and careful with his questions.

I soon realized that, on the way to the airport, Mr. Bond had been interviewing me. Having grown up near Spokane, spending years devouring the pages of the city's papers, I had learned a great deal about the town. Mr. Bond seemed to enjoy having me tag along. I welcomed the newcomers and made them feel at home in our city.

At the end of that day, one person was chosen from our group of high school students to serve as a student reporter on the Chronicle. I was the one chosen. I couldn't believe my good fortune. I was invited to spend my Saturdays on the rewrite desk, where I could mingle with the Chronicle reporters and learn the trade. My job was to work, watch and listen. I could hardly believe it was true.

My high school teachers were impressed and encouraged me to take on the job at the Chronicle, and at the same time to continue editing the school paper. It was an educational opportunity that I didn't fully realize at the time. I liked the idea because it was a paying job. By earning a real salary, I could start saving money. Even though I had fallen in love with the newspaper game, I was still dreaming of college, and becoming a teacher. I was eager to go to work and earn money.

But I knew I had a bigger task ahead of me. I had to convince my parents that I could do it. Our home at the ranch was 10 miles out of Cheney, and in order to work in Spokane, I had to find a way to get to Cheney and from Cheney to Spokane. I convinced my friend Nell McCall, to let me stay at her house on Friday nights.

I had known the McCall family since I was a child. Widowed when her children were very young, Nell's mother took in laundry to support her five children. The college professors, who all wore white dress shirts, were her customers. I offered to iron shirts in exchange for a place to spend the night.

With a solid plan, I was ready to ask my parents for permission to embark on my journalism career. I had everything all lined up. I hadn't lived 17 years under my father's roof not to know that I had to have a well laid plan if I was going to get his approval. When my parents agreed, I could hardly believe it. I was taking another step toward my goal.

Ernestine at the Chronicle rewrite desk

SPOKANE DAILY CHRONICLE.

County High School Students Help Edit Chronicle

Fourteen students from 12 high schools in the county school system came to Spokane Thursday and took one-day "jobs" as members of the Chronicle staff, just to show the regular force how to handle the work. Those taking part, from left to right, are: Front row—Ernestine McMillan, Cheney; Dorothy Burnett, Amber; Wilma Straughan, West Valley; Betty Waybright, Central Valley; Wilda Seehorn, Rockford; Dorothy Janson, Latah, and Mary Lee Wiggs, Otis Orchards. Rear row—Harold Byers, Valleyford; Harvey Raugust, Spangle; Bill Lewis, Milan; Jim Simpson, Otis Orchards; Harold Bockemeuhl, Deer Park, and John Paschall and Hamilton Hardin, Mead.

Article from Spokane Daily Chronicle

Pictured in Front row: Ernestine McMillan, Cheney; Dorothy Burnett, Amber; Wilma Straughan, West Valley; Betty Waybright, Central Valley; Wilda Seehorn, Rockford; Dorothy Janson, Latah; and Mary Lee Wiggs, Otis Orchards.

Rear row: Harold Byers, Valleyford; Harvey Raugust, Spangle; Bill Lewis, Milan; Jim Simpson, Otis Orchards; Harold Bockemeuhl, Deer Park, and John Paschall and Hamilton Hardin, Mead.

Byline

Every Saturday I did my best at the rewrite desk. Payday was Tuesday for the reporters who were paid $60 dollars a week. I got two dollars for each hour I worked, which was usually four hours. After taking out my train and bus fare, I put the rest in my bank account for college. I didn't write any big stories. That was for Mr. Bond and the other reporters. My job was to take the teletype stories from around the world and rewrite and condense them into filler.

I hung around the editor's desk. I wanted to be there when the phone rang in case Mr. Bond invited me to go along when the "Brass" came to town. We would meet them at the airport, with me acting as hostess, and get them settled in the hotel. We provided them with information about the town, making them feel at home. My years of going around with my nose in a book were paying off. I had accumulated a wealth of information about Spokane's history.

Sometimes when things were slow, I would write short articles about the town. One caught the eye of the City Editor and he published it in the paper. Sometimes, Myrtle Gaylord, who was editor of the Society Page, would need a little filler and she would put one of my poems in the paper.

One day at Cheney High School, I was sitting in study hall when I heard the fire alarm sound and fire engines rushing down the street. Peering out the window, I could see dark smoke pouring out of the downtown area. Quickly I signed out of study hall and raced down the street where I could see a huge fire burning in one of the oldest buildings in town.

Abe Brown's old livery stable on Main Street was on fire. It had been a busy place in earlier days when horses were a common sight. But with the popularity of the automobile it had been turned into a hay and feed store. The Brown family was one of the Cheney's pioneer families and now owned the largest car dealership in town. They were also engaged in developing the first real shopping center on Spokane's north side.

I rushed to a phone booth on the street across from the fire. I called the paper, got the City Editor on the line, and began to give him a blow by blow account of what was happening in my town.

"Send me a photographer!" I barked, like I heard the seasoned reporters say at the paper. "I've got a hot story here!"

Mr. Reilly must have laughed till his vest buttons popped. But he sent a photographer. Next I called the newspaper's morgue. I asked them to pull out all the pictures of the Brown family and send them up to the City Editor. Pronto! Then I got the City Desk on the line and dictated my story, as I stood in the phone booth across the street and watched the old livery stable go up in flames.

The photographer soon arrived and did his job. The morgue sent up pictures of the Brown family. I provided the historical background. All this as the local fire department battled to extinguish the flames. But the building went down, and a landmark vanished.

I heard the City Editor shout, "Hold the Press!" That meant I would make the front page. There were no sweeter words to any reporter's ears. Then I remembered that I was still in high school, and I scampered up the hill back to class. I waited around for the evening edition of the Chronicle to arrive on the six o'clock bus. Sure enough, there was my story on the front page, pictures and all. The byline read 'Ernestine McMillan.'

Having a front-page story was routine for some reporters, but it was a big event for me. A triumph that, along with a twenty-five dollar check, spurred me on to want to become a newspaper woman. As a result of the

Main Street Cheney circa 1946
Photograph courtesy of the Cheney Historical Museum

story, I was assigned as a reporter for the Northwest Sheet, with the city of Cheney and surrounding communities as my beat.

Women were rare in the newsroom. Most women reporters only worked the Society Page. If a story came up and a man was in the room, he got the assignment. Some days I sat at the rewrite desk all day. I was not accepted as a real reporter. It was partly my age, but mostly because I was a woman.

One day Rowland Bond took me to lunch at the Press Club. It happened after we had been on a long interview. It was well past noon when we headed back to the office. As we walked down the street, Bond suddenly took my arm and steered me straight into the Press Club just a few steps away.

"Let's get something to eat," said Bond.

"Mr. Bond," I said, "not in here. This is the Press Club!"

"Yeah," said Bond.

"But..." I said, hanging back. "I can't. No women allowed. You know that!"

"No women allowed, I've heard that," he said. "I say we give the boys a thrill."

We walked right in, straight up to the counter, where he ordered two hamburgers, a cup of coffee and a coke for me. Just like that. For a minute there was total silence. Finally a chair scraped against the floor and then voices resumed in the smoky room. The men returned to their conversations. Bond winked at me and took a big bite of his hamburger. We began going over the interview, comparing notes. Some of his reporter friends came by and he introduced me.

When we left the club and headed down the street to the Chronicle, Bond said, "You do a good job, kid. Those guys in there know it. They won't give you any trouble. They're just going to have to get used to you newspaper women."

FDR at Grand Coulee Dam

On October 2, 1937, President Franklin D. Roosevelt visited the construction site of Grand Coulee Dam. The dam was a massive public works project undertaken as part of Roosevelt's effort to ease joblessness during the Depression. Ground was broken on the dam in December of 1933 and it was finished in 1941.

The construction of Grand Coulee Dam was exactly the type of project that Roosevelt envisioned when he created the Public Works Administration in June of 1933. High unemployment gripped our little township as well as the rest of the nation. Joblessness stood at twenty-five percent. The dam project provided work for over six thousand men. Many people from our community left their farms and ranches in hope of a job on the dam. Now, FDR was coming to visit the project people were calling the 'Eighth Wonder of the World.'

Editor Newland Reilly included me in the group of reporters who would travel from Spokane to cover the story. A presidential visit was an important event. The reporters were called together and given strict instructions regarding our behavior. We were forbidden to mention, or even to suggest, that President Roosevelt was unable to walk. The country as a whole had heard little about him having polio.

President Roosevelt's bout with polio in 1920 had left him severely disabled. This had never been disclosed to the public. FDR was never photographed in a wheel chair or being helped by attendants. He was most often shown sitting down, riding in an automobile, or he would appear to be standing up with people crowded around him. Our Editor in Chief, as well as Mr. Crowley, the owner of the paper, made it very clear that none of our staff at the Spokane Chronicle was to reveal this information.

The dedication was such an important event that Father consented to drive us all to see the great dam. Although Father was a staunch Republican, he had respect for our national leaders, and I think he was pleased that I was part of the Press Corps chosen to cover the presidential visit.

Grandfather had been an advocate of the project all along, so he and Grandmother were included in our party. Grandfather was also eager to give us a tour of the Coulees. We crowded into the car before sunup that morning. With Father at the wheel, we drove out across the wheat fields of the Columbia Basin, on our way to see the Grand Coulee Dam and President Roosevelt.

We arrived at the dam, in the little town called Electric City to find the huge structure towering above us. I got out of the car and squirmed through the crowd to find the other reporters. Then we were escorted to an area near the top of the high structure where a platform loomed out over the great dam. From that high perch we could see the waters of the mighty Columbia River spilling over the dam. Reporters from newspapers around the country were gathered there, pencils ready, to hear the great man speak. I was so impressed at the sight of my hero, that I had a hard time keeping my mind on his speech. The day was unusually hot, so President Roosevelt kept his address brief.

Roosevelt spoke from a special platform, built with a ramp so that his car could be driven directly onto it. Addressing the crowd through loud speakers that were hooked up to his car, he called Grand Coulee Dam "a national undertaking" that was "doing a national good." The dam was not only providing employment to people in the immediate area, but also to thousands of people in factories across the country that were providing steel and other materials for the dam.

"We think of this as something that is benefiting this part of the country primarily," He said. "But we must also remember that one half of the total cost of this dam is paid to the factories east of the Mississippi River."

He marveled at the wonderful progress made since his first visit, three years earlier. He also implied that the entire Columbia Basin project would be completed as planned. He predicted that millions of acres of new land would be irrigated, providing homes and livelihoods for the farmers who had been displaced by the dustbowl.

"You young people especially are going to live to see the day when thousands and thousands of people are going to use this great lake both for transportation purposes and for pleasure purposes. There will be sail boats and motor boats and steamship lines running from here to the northern border of the United States and into Canada."

"I am always glad to see a project in the construction stage because when it is finished very few people will realize — they won't be able to visualize — all the difficult work in the actual construction. I hope to come back here in another two or three years and see this dam pretty nearly completed. When that time comes, I think we had better, all of us, have a reunion of rejoicing." (excerpts from: Franklin D. Roosevelt, Remarks at Grand Coulee Dam, October 2, 1937.)

His remarks reinforced my grandfather's vision of the future. Grandfather was an ardent supporter of the Coulee Dam Project. He had read all the news articles about the dam. He believed it would bring water to the dry lands above the river. He understood the scope and depth of the project, and told us all in sweeping detail, how all the sun-scorched sandy desert would become a farmer's paradise, once the waters were harnessed. I hoped that Grandfather could hear what his hero was saying.

Rowland Bond managed to push to the front and speak directly to the President. I was just so thrilled to stand where I was and look at him. I was so close I could see the color of his red tie and his smiling eyes under his hat. I was so star-struck that it never occurred to me to move forward to shake his hand.

When the ceremony was over, I made my way back through the crowd to my family. We drove up out of the crowd that swarmed around the dam to the top of the hill. Father found a winding road that took us away from the river and out through the canyons to the bluffs that shaded us from the afternoon sun. It was late in the day when we turned back toward home.

All afternoon, Grandfather spun his yarns about the days of his youth when he came to these very canyons to round up wild horses. He told us about those early days of the 1880s when he was a young man growing up on the Breaks of the Snake River on Montgomery Ridge in Asotin County, Washington.

He had his eye on a pretty little gal named Mattie Hollenback whom he soon married. He came to know and admire her father, Cornelius Hollenback, who had lived the life of a cowboy during the days of the great cattle drives. Great Grandfather Hollenback had ridden the western prairies with Buffalo Bill. He had been a cowhand on the famous Santa Fe and Chisholm Trails and then brought his family west on the Oregon Trail.

As we drove along, Grandfather told about the beautiful wild horses he had seen here. He explained that in the days of his youth, there were great herds of magnificent ponies living on the grasses that grew beside the streams flowing out of the many lakes in the coulees. How swift those ponies were. They would throw up their heads and listen, then snort and flee up the rocky walls of the coulees, their tails flying as they sought safety in some hidden canyon. Grandfather's stories were so real that we almost expected to see wild ponies as we drove through the tall rocky canyon.

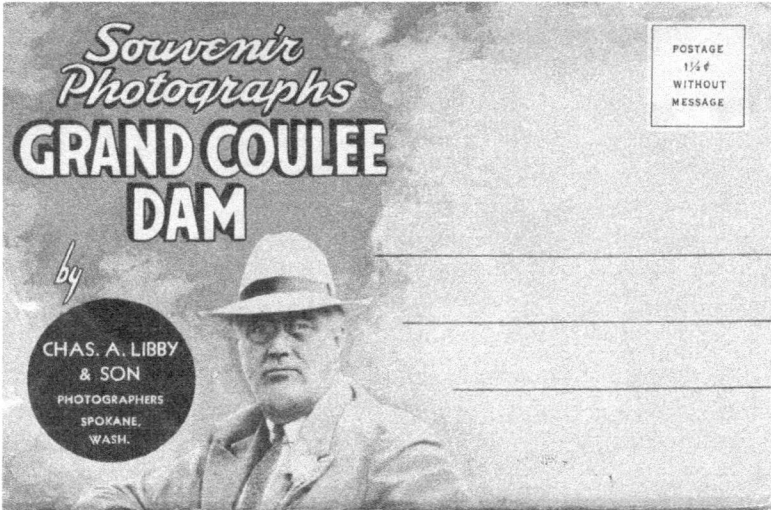

Souvenir Photograph, FDR at Grand Coulee Dam

Souvenir Photograph Grand Coulee Dam

Turnbull National Wildlife Refuge

The Turnbull National Wildlife Refuge was established in 1937 by an Executive Order of President Franklin D. Roosevelt. Located within the Pacific Flyway, the refuge included deep permanent sloughs and seasonal potholes and marshes. It was an important habitat for migrating and breeding waterfowl. Every year, birds traveled from Canada to Patagonia in spring and fall, heading to breeding grounds, or travelling to overwintering sites. Waterfowl stopped to rest in the many marshes, wetlands, and lakes south of Cheney. It was the perfect location for a wildlife refuge.

For decades, the meadows and wetlands of the scablands had been farmed. They furnished the natural hay crop for horses and dairy cows in the region. Many farmers on these little hay ranches were barely scratching out a living. The federal project would encompass about sixteen thousand acres of meadows and wetlands south of Cheney. It would affect many of the farms there. The project was only in its first phase, and the Spokane Chronicle was ready to present the project to the community.

In 1938, while I was a senior in high school, Newland Reilly, the editor of the Chronicle, offered me the job of covering the Turnbull Refuge project for the paper. It fell within my beat on the Northwest Sheet and affected dozens of farmers in the Cheney area. It was an important assignment. I was so excited when Mr. Reilly came to me and listed all the reasons he was offering me the assignment. I was a country girl who had grown up on a scabland farm. I had a keen interest in local history. I was interested in and could identify the birds in the region. My father was a recognized conservation farmer. And more importantly, I was well acquainted with most of the farmers whose land would be involved in the project.

In preparation, I met with the sponsors of the project, the representatives of the Department of the Interior, local and state Game and Wildlife people, as well as state politicians and others who supported the plan. Since the refuge was created by executive order of the president, there was no question that it was going to happen, regardless of local concerns. Proponents saw it as a needed resting place for waterfowl that migrated the length of the continent, particularly Canada geese and the trumpeter swan.

Turnbull National Wildlife Refuge
Photo by Alison Hilton 2011

The project began by buying out many of the small scabland farms and ranches in the wetland area. To many farmers, who were barely hanging on, this came as a great boon. But not all of the farmers were in agreement. One of the farmers most seriously affected by the refuge plan was Bert Findley, the father of my very best friend, Clare. His property contained many ponds and wetlands. I did not know what position he would take regarding the project. He was a dairyman and greatly respected for his prize Holstein cattle.

My father had purchased many calves from Mr. Findley over the years and the two men had great respect for one another. Father suggested that I call on Mr. Findley and explain my interest in the project. I gathered my courage and went to talk with him. He was very kind and encouraging. He knew that someone had to report on the refuge story and he believed I would present a fair account of the project.

My first article brought me some recognition among my fellow reporters. The story was important enough that the paper assigned me a photographer, and the article was given a full-page spread, complete with photographs and my own byline to begin the series. It appeared on the front page of the Northwest Sheet. The articles I wrote about Turnbull were divided into several installments and appeared over many months.

As the government began to acquire the land, the project became controversial. Landowners were not always willing to surrender their property, regardless of the price offered. However, times were tough and some farmers sold willingly, glad to be rid of marginal farms. Others held out until the last possible moment and gave in only because the government could condemn their property through the power of eminent domain.

Some farmers, including Mr. Findley hired lawyers to negotiate for them. They secured the best prices for their acreage. Over several years, the land was acquired. Families moved off their farms and the Turnbull National Wildlife Refuge was established. The home and outbuildings of the Findley Farm became the headquarters for the refuge.

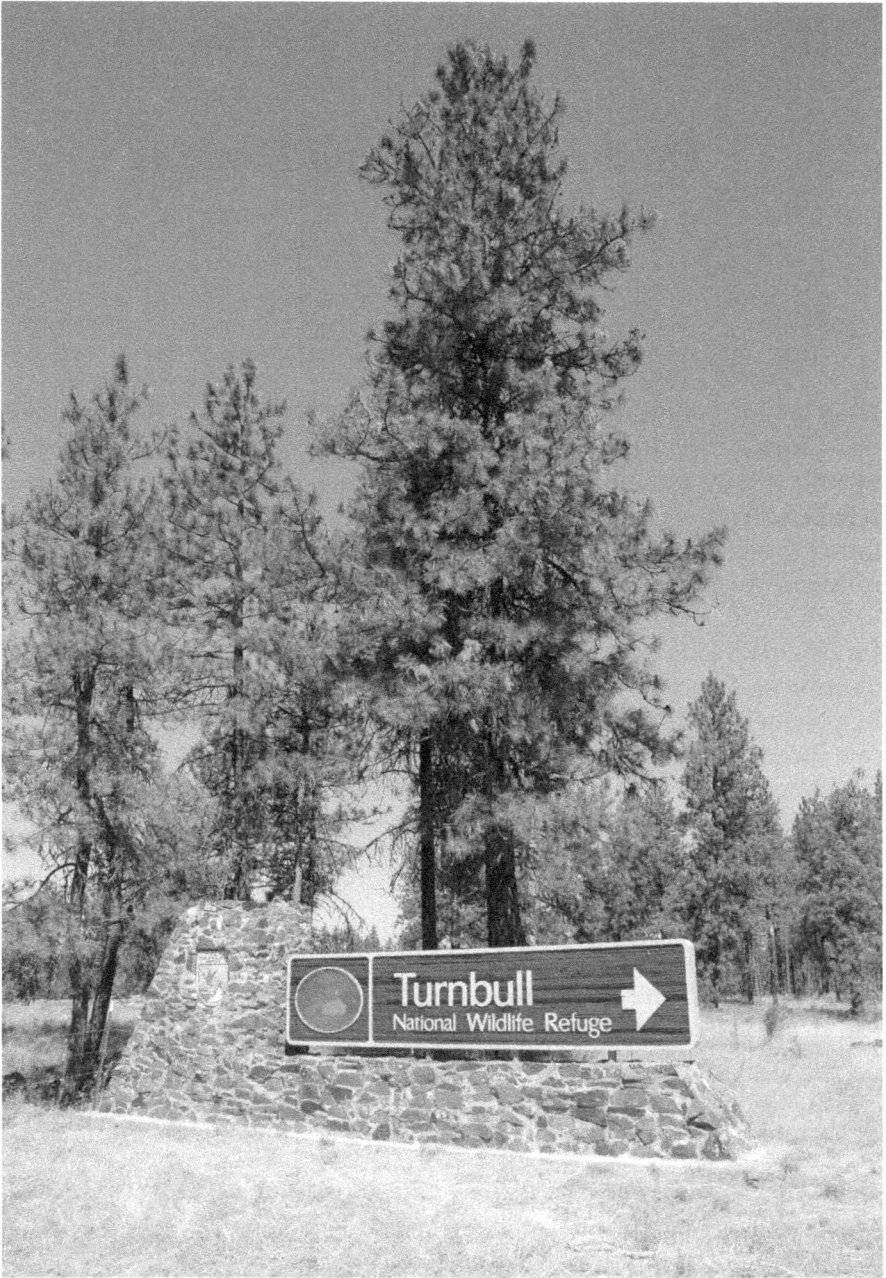

Turnbull National Wildlife Refuge Entrance
Photo by Alison Hilton 2011

Dashed Hopes and Dreams

High school graduation was just one week away when disaster struck. I had known for a long time that if I was to go on to college, I would have to find a way to finance my education myself. I desperately needed a scholarship. I worked hard to get straight A's through high school. My father worked hard but could barely make ends meet. I knew there was no money set aside for college. My teachers all knew my situation.

I was working as a community news correspondent on the Spokane Daily Chronicle. I spent every Saturday at the re-write desk where I was paid by the inch of print I wrote. I was successful as a reporter, even earning one hundred dollars for one of my stories. Every cent I earned went into my college fund in the Cheney Bank. I never passed up an opportunity to work. But even all my savings would not begin to pay my way through college.

Cheney High School awarded one full scholarship each year to Eastern Washington College. The scholarship was given to the student who finished top in the graduating class. I believed I was number one in the class so I was counting on receiving the scholarship. I was working in the high school office one day, honing my skills, just in case all else failed and I needed to find work as a secretary. That morning, the school superintendent C. J. Cooil came out of his office.

"Come in and sit down a minute," he said, pointing to a chair in his office. "I am so sorry to have to tell you this." He paused and I steeled myself. I thought perhaps someone had died.

He cleared his throat and went on. "The school board has decided to disregard the importance of grades this year. Instead, they have decided that the valedictorian and salutatorian will be selected by the board rather than based on class standing. This means that, regardless of grades, the honors and the scholarship will go to two students determined by the board. Since you are top of the class, you will be able to give your speech as part of the graduation program, but the scholarship money has been given to someone else."

I sat there stunned, staring down at my hands, as my world went to pieces. The bright future that I had worked so hard for had been just a castle in the air. I had known all along that it was up to me to find a way to finance college. I had worked so hard and now all my dreams lay in ashes at my feet. Faced with such a blow, I was unable to speak. Without a word, I left the room.

Word spread fast. No doubt the faculty had heard about the school board's decision earlier. They only waited until I had been told. Mr. Pierson, my biology teacher, called me to his classroom. There I found him tight-lipped, pacing back and forth behind his desk. He stopped, looked me straight in the eye, and spoke to me in a strained voice.

"This is outrageous," he declared. "Ernestine, we will see to it that you get to go to college."

Mr. Pierson sent me down to talk to my family doctor, Dr. West. Having taken care of me since childhood, he too had heard the news. He remained calm, but I could tell that he was genuinely upset.

"You deserved that scholarship," the doctor said. "There are folks who will help with this. We are going to see to it that you go to college."

He gave me a hug and sent me down to talk to Dr. Bernard, who was a dentist. He was also a member of the Washington State Game Commission. He was the person who had been instrumental in getting the Turnbull project underway. He knew that the stories I had written about the refuge for the Spokane Chronicle had been helpful in gaining local support for the project.

"There are people at the state level who will be able to help you," he said.

Even with the assurances of the community leaders and businessmen, I went home that night and crawled into bed with Edith and cried myself to sleep.

Values and Ideals

Living at the Drake Place was difficult for Mother. She was often depressed and unhappy. With no telephone to keep in touch with her friends and neighbors, she felt isolated and out of touch with the world. Bogged down with work and worry, she didn't go to town for weeks at a time. She crated the eggs and sent them to town with me when I drove to school. I traded them for groceries from a list she gave me.

As for me, school had been everything. It was my final year in high school, busy and hectic. I liked my classes and my teachers inspired me. Despite the hard times at home, I managed to keep my grades up. I took part in many school activities, even playing the piano for pep rallies and editing the school annual. I had my work at the Chronicle on Saturdays. I drove us all back and forth to school.

But now, after the stunning blow I had been dealt at school, it seemed to me that my graduation would be a fiasco. My valedictory speech, which was to be a triumphant acceptance of my scholarship, was entitled *Values and Ideals*. But now it seemed like a cruel joke to have to stand before my fellow graduates and give that speech.

Everything I worked for was gone. I didn't know where to turn. My heart was broken, and I felt the void opening before me. For the first time in my life, I felt defeated and afraid to look forward. Although I knew that Mother was badly burdened and unhappy, I had to talk to her about what had happened.

"This has been a serious setback for you," she told me as she held me and stroked my hair. "Your graduation speech is good. Now is your time to put your values and ideals to the test. Stand up for what you believe, and when you speak, everyone in town will be with you."

Graduation night came, and it was not as bad as I had expected. Wayne Swegle, the salutatorian spoke first and the audience responded with polite applause. When it was time for my speech, I felt calm. I stepped to the lectern, and with my eyes on my family, I poured out my thoughts. The audience clapped and cheered and stood for an ovation. Pride and satisfaction filled my heart.

Ernestine McMillan
High school graduation 1938

COMMENCEMENT

THURSDAY, JUNE 2, 1938 - - 8:00 P. M.
Superintendent C. J. Cooil Presiding

Processional	Class of 1938
Invocation	Reverend Adams
"Break O' Day"	Sanderson
Josephine Carey, Alto	
Betty Mickey, Accompanist	
Salutatory	Wayne Swegle
Values and Ideals	Ernestine McMillan
"Deep River"	Negro Spiritual
Barbara Stronach	
Betty Mickey, Accompanist	
Economic Security	Bert Llewellyn
Education for Physical Security	Margaret Murray
"Giannina mia"	Friml
"The Star"	Rogers
Triple Trio	
Marilyn Newton, Phyllis Edgington, Ruby Morrow, Barbara Stronach, Anne Edgington, Ruth Van Brunt, Marjorie Cutting, Esthernel McCall, Maxine Carr. Betty Mickey, Accompanist	
Fair Play	Jerry Randall
Valedictory	Betty Mickey
"Dedication"	Franz
"Diaphenia"	Rickett
Glen Conley, Baritone	
Betty Mickey, Accompanist	
Special Awards	Mr. Cooil
Presentation of the Class	Mr. Gardner
Presentation of Diplomas	Mr. Mickey
	(Chairman of Board)
Recessional	Glee Clubs

NOTE: The audience will remain seated until the seniors have marched out.

Commencement Program
June 1938

The next day was Saturday and Earl came to see me, and we went for a ride. "Show me the little creek you talk about from when you were a kid," Earl said when we got into his pickup. So we drove down the old road toward Tyler. We parked, and walked through the woods from the backside of the Green Meadow until we came to the upper waters of the little creek.

It was cool there among the green mosses and hidden violets that blossomed along its trickling water. There was no wind and the leaves of the quaking aspen trees were still. When we came to the big rocky bluff that marked the end of the meadow, we climbed up to where the wild syringa bloomed, its heady perfume filling the air. Earl cut off a branch of the sweet white flowers for me to hold, and took my picture.

"This is your graduation picture from me," he said.

Ernestine McMillan
Earl took this picture as a graduation gift for me.

It was a quiet, happy day. I was glad that Earl had come to see me. It was fun to show him where I had been a little girl, how we had played in the creek and made our playhouses. It put a happy ending to my high school days. There beside the bubbling creek, I saw myself no longer as a child, but a woman with my whole life ahead of me. I was 18, a grownup, and my future was up to me. Walking beside the creek with Earl, thinking of all the changes that had taken place in my life, seemed to anchor me. Here at the edge of 'has been' and 'would be,' I found myself again. Whatever might happen, I knew I would find my way. How wise and sweet of Earl to bring me here.

On Sunday after graduation, Mother made a nice dinner with one of her pretty cakes. I invited Clare to spend the day with us, and we celebrated our graduation. I tried my best to look ahead. Clare and I were making plans to take summer classes at the college. Then, a dark cloud descended on our celebration. Mr. Drake arrived during dinner, spoiling our little party. He insisted that Father go out in the field with him to discuss some business. Father looked both furious and defeated as he put his fork down.

After Clare went home, I went upstairs and cried. Mother came up to console me. It was then that she told me of her plan to get us out of this place before Father's health was ruined. He was ill and tired, yet he refused to see the doctor. Mother knew that Father must find something he could look forward to. She was writing letters and looking for a way out.

It was a week after our graduation that I was called to come to see Mr. Pierson in his classroom. There I met Mr. Bert Oliver from the Vocational Education Department in Olympia. Dr. West was there and so was Dr. Bernard, the dentist. Mr. Oliver presented me with a four year scholarship to Eastern Washington College of Education.

My dream was coming true after all. But I managed to hold my happy tears long enough to thank Mr. Oliver and his department for their generosity. And also to thank the three men who had made it all possible. The scholarship carried one stipulation. I was required to spend one year teaching in the state of Washington. I happily gave them my promise to work very hard and be the best teacher they ever saw. I knew that I owed a great debt to those men.

Mother Finds a Way Out

Clare and I found a small apartment in Cheney so we could attend summer school at college. I boxed up my things at the Drake Place and took them to the apartment. Clare and I had fun setting up our first home. We found a shelf for our books and brought our favorite blankets for our bed. We each brought a few dishes for the tiny shelf that served as our china cupboard. We had two pans for use on our hot plate and a piece of oilcloth for the table. The table served, not only for meals, but also a place to study. When one of us was writing at the table by the window, the other could stretch out on the bed and read.

Out at the Drake Place my family struggled and Mother was looking for a change. She learned that the Bohle Place, located near the intersection of Graham and Salnave Roads, was vacant. She wrote to the owners and they agreed to rent it to her. My family could pull up stakes, get away, and go back to the old neighborhood. When Mother told Father of her plan, he put up no argument.

"Go ahead," he said. "We aren't getting anywhere here." And he went to bed.

Mr. Drake was notified that they were leaving. Plans were made quickly, and two weeks later they packed up and moved to a tiny house on just eighty acres. Mother called it "a place to squat." I never lived with my family on the Bohle Place. She wrote me, "With ten heifers and our household things, we left Mr. Drake with his lap full of cows!"

Father never knew that Mother had also written a letter to our old friend, Mr. Mickey, explaining their situation, and asking if he could find a way to give Father some work. Mr. Mickey came for a visit. He asked Father to come to work for him on the harvest crew. Father was very pleased, and agreed to take the job. Father stood a little straighter and there was a look of pride on his face as he watched Mr. Mickey drive away down the road.

Mr. Mickey loaned Father his truck to move their belongings. Don and Ted drove the cows up the Salnave Road to the new place. Mother put her hens in a crate and sent them along with the furniture to the little house. There was no chicken house, so she penned off a corner in the barn and set up some apple boxes for their nests. The house was very small, but no one seemed to mind. They were free of the tightfisted Mr. Drake and out on their own again.

Mother's first act in the new place was to order one hundred baby chicks. When they arrived she placed them in boxes and gave them hot water bottles to huddle around. At night she brought them into the house in cardboard boxes and placed them behind the stove to keep warm. When they grew to fryer size, she moved them into the old garage. She saved ninety-nine out of that one hundred chicks. She was back in the chicken business. When all else failed, the egg money would keep our family going.

Determined to make a new start, Father was pleased to be part of Mr. Mickey's crew. He was soon feeling much better and was busy getting the combines ready for the harvest in the summer ahead. Edith began working for the Mickey family too. She got a job at the cookhouse that summer with Mrs. Mickey. 12 year-old Teddy got a job shocking hay for a farmer in the Lance Hills. Don stayed home to help Mother with the new place. In his spare time, Don got a job doing chores at the Spence dairy barn. The McMillan family was back on its feet.

Father Goes Back to His Roots

In no time at all, my family was settled in again in our old neighborhood. Mother was calling up all her old friends and they gabbed away on the telephone. The Spokane Chronicle came daily to the mailbox on Salnave Road. Mother tended her chickens. Father had only two cows to milk and one calf to feed. Don and Ted often took care of that chore. Father's health began to improve.

Everybody was happy again. Clare and I were busy with our college lives. I worked at the Chronicle on Saturdays, and tried to spend Sunday with my family. Mother had immediately planted a garden, and soon there were fresh vegetables. Of course, there were plenty of chores at the little ranch. One day, when harvest was only a few weeks away, Father came up with a surprise.

"How would you all like to take a trip?" he asked one Sunday afternoon, when we all were lounging on the porch.

We couldn't believe our ears. Father was suggesting we take a trip. He rarely ever left the ranch. He was the man who considered going to town for supplies a wasted work day. He never left the ranch to visit anyone except Grandfather and Grandmother. We were excited and asked what he had in mind.

"I have been thinking of taking you kids down to see Montgomery Ridge," he said. "We could have Bill Spence milk the cows while we're gone. If Sis could take a weekend off, we could go down to see where I grew up."

"Do you really mean that?" Mother asked.

"Write Edna and Wes and tell them we are coming for a visit next weekend," Father said. "I'm sure they will put us up. We'll go down to the Ridge, and I will show you where I lived when I was a boy. Then we'll go up to Cloverland where Mother and I first met."

Our Father was back to his old happy self. Before long, we might even hear him singing again. The very idea of Father suggesting a trip just for fun meant that anything could happen. A date was set, the second weekend in June. Mother called Aunt Edna on the telephone and told her of our plans, and right away she invited us to come spend the weekend with them.

The drive down through the ripening fields of grain in the Palouse was spectacular. At Steptoe, Father turned off the highway and drove the car up the most twisting road, around and around to the very top of Steptoe Butte. Mother lingered in the car, she never liked heights, but Father coaxed her out and we all gazed at the spectacular view below. Gentle winds blew waving fields of grain that were spread out below like a patchwork quilt. As we walked about on the rim of the hill, Father talked to us about its history. It was the site of skirmishes between the whites and the Indians.

He recalled for us a visit he had made on horseback to a Lodge that was built on the top of the hill where visitors stopped on their way from Walla Walla to Colville in northern Washington years and years ago. The lodge was long gone, burned to the ground in a spectacular fire many years ago.

We returned to the highway and traveled on to the top of the Lewiston hill. Again we got out of the car, peered down over the rim of the hill and gazed at the highway below. It looked like a snake as it coiled back and forth as it wound down the steep Lewiston Grade to the Clearwater River below. Spread out before us like a map, we saw the two rivers, the Clearwater and the Snake come together, marking the boundary between Idaho and Washington.

Lewiston Hill was steep and full of twists and turns, so Father drove cautiously down the winding grade into the town of Lewiston, Idaho. Driving slowly down its main street, Father told us more tales from his youth when he knew everyone in town. Soon we came to the crossing of the Snake River that brought us back into the State of Washington at Clarkston.

Lewiston Hill in background
Lewiston, Idaho and Clarkston, Washington in foreground

The hills, shaped by the mighty rivers that came together there, formed a backdrop for the town. From the center of town, we drove along the Snake River on our way to Asotin. On the route we were excited to see "The Swallow's Nest." Father had often spoken of this big rock beside the river. It stood higher than a ten story building. Plastered on its face were thousands of bird nests. Swallows swarmed over it. Some were feeding their young, some were building their nests.

No. 4- Swallow's Nest Rock on Snake River.
The nesting place of Myriads of Swallows
until driven away by blasting.

Swallow's Nest Rock, 1907
On Snake River near Lewiston, Idaho

In Asotin we drove past the little nursing home where Edith and I were born. Then Father showed us the McMillan family home near the center of town, and Great Grandfather Hollenback's barn down by the river.

Soon we turned up another winding hillside road. Now we were on our way to Montgomery Ridge, the place where father grew up. We passed the little hamlet of Anatone and continued on Montgomery Ridge Road for several miles. He stopped the car at the top of the ridge and we walked to the rim of the hill.

From there Father pointed out to us, far below in the canyon, the little white house and the red barn nestled in a cove in the Snake River hills. The poplar trees planted by his mother many years ago still stood tall between the house and the barn. The hills sheltered a little farmyard. We sat in the grass on the rim of the canyon, taking in the smell of sage and wildflowers blooming in the warm June air. Father told about the time he and his little sister Mamie tied their wagon to their pony's tail and rode around the canyon rim. His terrified mother saw them, ran out and put a stop to their prank.

**McMillan homestead on Montgomery Ridge
where Father was born and grew up**

From then on, whenever Father told us stories of growing up on the Breaks of the Snake River we would remember that June day when he showed us all the places of his boyhood home. We drove back to Asotin. Then we went up an even scarier hill to the little village of Cloverland. Mother pointed out the sights of the small town where she had grown up. We saw the store and post office and the little schoolhouse where she went to school.

We listened quietly as Father told us once again how our parents met. We had heard the story many times, but now we had seen the places for ourselves. Years ago, one of the ways that country boys and girls got together was at a picnic social. The older girls would each make a picnic dinner and decorate her basket with ribbons and garlands. Then there would be an auction. Bidding often involved teasing, joking, and competition. The high bidder for each basket, usually a suitor, would then get to eat the supper with its maker.

Father had taken a shine to 15 year-old, Myrtle Marks of Cloverland. She was a pretty redhead who caught his eye. At the social, he waited for Mother's basket to come up for auction and made an extravagant bid that no one could top. They ate the supper together and fell in love. They were married a year later on May 10, 1916 at the Lewiston Hotel.

We spent the night at Uncle Wes and Aunt Edna's farm. Father and Uncle Wes and the boys all slept in the barn. It was like old times. The next day we all went down to the park beside the Snake River where our families gathered for a picnic.

There beside the river, Father and his brothers and sisters shared stories of how the family came to Washington State from Wisconsin and Minnesota over the Oregon Trail, and settled down on Montgomery Ridge. Stories were told about the glory days when the McMillan Clan lived in Scotland. The tale was told of the McMillans settling in upstate New York, where they fought in the Revolutionary War. Then gradually, over many years, they came west over the Oregon Trail.

We met aunts and uncles and cousins of the McMillan family, not only Uncle Wes and Aunt Edna and our cousins Delmar, Elton and Keith, but Father's brother Arthur and Aunt Grace, and our cousins Elma and Erma. We also met father's sister Nellie and our cousins Dale and Ilene.

It was agreed that the McMillan and Hollenback families would gather there by the river every year for a reunion on the second Sunday in June. Life turned around for us that day, when Father was reunited with his McMillan family.

McMillan Family Picnic by the Snake River

Left to right: Cousin Erma, Cousin Sophia, Aunt Grace, Aunt Mary, Cousin Rollie McMillan, Father - Ernest McMillan

Summer Semester and the Incredible Man

One week after graduating from high school, with my scholarship in hand, I entered Eastern Washington College of Education for the summer semester. Clare and I had rented an upstairs two-by-four apartment listed under "Housekeeping Rooms for Rent." It was on 2nd Street not far from campus. We shared the upstairs bathroom with an older lady whose canary woke us every morning, and a newlywed couple who woke us late at night.

Having known each other since childhood, Clare and I got along fine. She too was serious about her studies. For our course work I chose elementary education. Clare wished to teach high school students. We both chose art, history, and composition. But she chose French and I kept to my love of journalism.

It was our first time away from home and we loved our place. Despite all its faults, it was the symbol of our independence. I earned my share of the rent writing for the Spokane Chronicle. We cooked our food on a hot plate, went to classes in the morning and spent the afternoons in the library. Being country girls, we missed the outdoors, and in the evenings we often tramped the hills and fields that surrounded the campus.

During that summer I tried to imagine what kind of teacher I would be. With teachers back for the summer session, I was confronted daily with walking examples. Sitting next to those experienced professionals I learned many things. I listened in shamelessly on their conversations and heard what the classroom was really like. I knew that I had much to learn.

I dove into college life like a swimmer and came up happy and eager. My days spilled over into nights when I poured over my books. My first year composition class was my favorite and I was inspired by Professor Ralph Allen. I began trying serious writing on my own. This writing was very different from the succinct wording used on the newspaper. Careful thought and imagination was necessary. I poured word to paper with a new zeal.

On Saturdays I worked at the Chronicle. While Clare slept in, I crept out of bed and caught the 7:10 am train into Spokane. The trip cost me twenty-five cents. I returned home on the 5:15 pm bus for fifteen cents. Clare was a sleepyhead and could not appreciate how much I enjoyed that twenty-minute train ride. She would lie in bed with the covers over her head and groan at me for interrupting her sleep. But I was eager to go to work. I would grab my hat and race the five blocks to the train station.

I worked on the Chronicle at the rewrite desk. No one else on the paper wanted anything to do with the job. However, I stuck with it, knowing I was honing my writing skills. I sat beside the desk of the City Editor and watched the news pour in over the teletype. I condensed the stories down to a few lines to be used as fillers in the paper. When it came time to put the paper to bed, the Editor would call to me, 'Give me an inch," or "I need two and a half inches" – whatever was needed to fill the space at the end of a big story. I prided myself on always having something ready for him when he called.

Sometimes, if a reporter came in with a exciting story, the editor would shout, "Hold the press!" to the man upstairs. It was exciting when that happened and made me think I would enjoy a career in journalism.

The Chronicle was an afternoon paper. It came off the press at noon and was on the streets soon afterward. It was mailed out as an evening paper. The two story high presses could be seen from the sidewalk through large windows. City Editor, Newland Reilly, would stand at the bottom of the press and grab the first page that came off, checking to see that everything was right. On Saturday, it was a thrill to watch the bright and colorful Sunday funnies come off the big presses.

Clare and I were independent women, out on our own that wonderful idyllic summer. Even though we lived off campus in our own apartment, we had to live under strict college dormitory rules. We were required to check in and out. Curfew required us to be in by ten o'clock during the week and by midnight Saturday and Sunday nights.

Every once in awhile, I would come in late and find the door locked. I had no recourse but to run the ten blocks up the hill in the dark to my friend Nell McCall's house and crawl into bed with her. For their hospitality I would iron shirts for her mother.

Even under the strict house rules, it was a lovely time. Removed from the many farm chores at home, for the first time in my life, I had time for myself. Although Clare and I were both very busy and in a great hurry all the time, we were proud of our new independence and enjoyed the sweet freedom of being out on our own.

We had little money between us. We depended on my mother's delicious home-baked bread and fresh eggs, milk and cream from the Findley farm, and other leftovers our mothers sent back with us from Sunday visits. I had learned to cook in my childhood, but Clare was raised in a home with household help and didn't know how to boil an egg or make a cup of coffee.

Clare and I referred to Earl as the Incredible Man. He was working at the Cheney Creamery. The Creamery was located at Main Street and College Avenue. It was owned and operated by Milton Hunt. It sold milk and cream as well as butter and its own Cheney Sun-Glo ice cream. We made unashamed visits there to see him, where Earl would hand out pats of butter and pints of ice cream whose battered cartons made them unsuitable for the store. Between Earl's creamery donations and our mothers' leftovers, Clare and I were eating pretty regularly.

Earl had bought a flashy red pick-up truck. He was easy to spot driving down the street. When he came to pick me up, I'd find him parked on the street in front of our apartment. leaning casually against the fender of his red truck looking handsome and suave. Then we'd go off to the movies or out for a drive in his shiny new rig.

Earl and I loved sitting out on the campus lawn under the trees, reading books to each other, soaking in the peaceful atmosphere of the college and basking in our love for each other. Our favorite spot was under an ancient elm by the Kissing Rock near the old church on the corner of the campus. We teased that someday we might get married there.

We kept those days as carefree as possible. The war loomed over us. Earl was such a kind and gentle person. The prospect of being asked to take a life in war bothered him terribly. He couldn't imagine himself in that situation and he worried over it constantly.

Earl was eager to get on with his life. He was serious about his studies in math and bacteriology that would be helpful in the dairy business that he hoped to share with his father. I too had my worries. I took every job opportunity and hoarded my money as I looked eagerly toward my teaching certificate. I was grateful every day to the three men who had secured my scholarship, and I felt deeply obligated to fulfill my agreement with them.

Our apartment house in Cheney on 2nd Street

Clare Findley

Ernestine McMillan

Starving Students

A great many changes were taking place for my family when Father went to work for Mr. Mickey. The summer of 1938 I started college and lived in town. When harvest was over, my family moved to a ranch in the Lance Hills owned by Mr. Mickey.

When the fall semester arrived, Clare and I gave up our little apartment and joined the freshman class of commuter students. She drove her car from home and I went back to my parents. I soon found that this wasn't going to work out. The ranch was south of Cheney. It was a mile hike up and down two steep hills to catch the bus. In the winter it would be difficult. My classes were earlier than the bus schedule. When there was an outbreak of Scarlet Fever in the neighborhood, I stopped riding the bus and went to stay in the McCall household.

Mrs. McCall was a widow with five children, four daughters and one son, Kenny, who was my age. We had known the family for many years. Mrs. McCall took in washing. She and her daughters washed and ironed shirts for college professors. I enjoyed using the electric irons, and liked ironing. There were always piles of shirts in the baskets.

My Camp Fire Group met every Thursday night after school. I was invited to spend that night with Mrs. Cutting's daughter, Marjorie, who was Edith's age. Mr. Cutting worked nights at the flour mill, and we had evenings to ourselves, to study, play games or music. Mother and Father sometimes came to town on Fridays, and I could go home with them for the weekend.

There was a room at the college especially assigned for the commuter students. We could gather there in the morning before class, and safely leave our books, coats, and belongings. We frequently met there to eat our sack lunches. We were appropriately dubbed the "Starving Students."

Some of us had scholarships, but all of us had to buy our own books, pay for our own housing and find some way to make ends meet. First year students were not allowed to work for the professors, but I found that I could augment my slim income by typing term papers for other students. I was thankful for the typing skills I had learned in high school. I didn't own a typewriter, but my journalism teacher, Howard Holmquist, allowed me to use the office typewriter, where I pounded the keys into the wee hours of the morning.

Clothes became a problem for me. My wardrobe was very slim. I had just three dresses, a navy blue cotton with white collar and cuffs, a red plaid with pleated skirt and a green print. I had two skirts, a black one and a brown one, two white blouses and a red sweater. I did not have a coat, but made myself a jacket from an old coat someone gave mother. When it rained I just ran faster.

Although I was a freshman, I was allowed to choose an advanced journalism class due to my work experience on the Chronicle. Soon I was given a spot on the staff of the college newspaper, and by the second semester I was the editor. This was exciting work for me. I loved my journalism teacher. Professor Holmquist was a big burly old fellow in baggy tweeds, with a battered old felt hat that he kept jammed down over his head. He had been a war correspondent in the First World War and typed wildly with one finger.

The college paper was called *The Journal*. It was printed at the Cheney Free press office downtown. The Cheney Free Press had the only linotype machine in town. Issues of the paper required careful reading and correction before they were ready to be set in type, and printed. The first thing a journalism student had to learn was how to read and correct the galley sheets.

I picked up the process quickly and liked doing it. But I didn't relish working downtown at night. The only time the college paper could use the linotype was after the Cheney Free Press had been put to bed.

The galleys were started late in the day, and it was always far into the night before they were ready. That meant that I would often find myself running up to 7th Street in the middle of the night to the McCall's house. Rushing alone through the windswept night, I often arrived breathless and frightened.

Main Street Cheney Circa 1947
Photograph courtesy of the Cheney Historical Museum

Because I had started college during summer quarter, I finished my freshman requirements early. I became a sophomore at the start of spring quarter. Moving up a class gave me increased privileges and I was eligible to work for a professor.

I went to work for a young history professor. I was a good typist and a great proofreader. I typed his letters and the speeches and lectures he gave on other campuses. I also kept his office neat so that he could find things when he needed them. For this I was paid the princely sum of $10 a month. That salary meant that I could now afford to buy lunch in the cafeteria. With daily lunches and the candy bars that Earl kept in his locker, I left the ranks of the starving students.

I continued as editor of the college paper for a second year. I especially enjoyed my classes in composition. Ralph Allen, my professor, was very encouraging. In one of my comp classes, we decided to publish a booklet of our own poems and stories. We dubbed it *The Writers' Cramp*. It was an opportunity for first-time writers to appear in print. We had fun with the project. Articles were submitted and each selection carefully edited. My newspaper skills helped put the little book together, and I was proud to have a story and some poetry of my own included.

Staff of the college newspaper, The Journal
Last in line is Professor Holmquist, front is Ernestine

I still had no home on campus. I seldom went home to the Lance Hills farm, but sometimes I'd ride there on the school bus with Don and Ted if I got out of class early enough. The McCall family always took me in when I had to stay in town late. I was a Camp Fire Guardian to a group of little girls and could always spend Thursday night at the welcoming home of my Camp Fire leader, Lulu Cutting.

Girls in the dorms were not allowed to have overnight guests, but once in a while their friendly housemother would let me stay the night with my good friend, Woody Johnson, in the Senior Hall Dormitory. That flock of girls in Senior Hall helped me so often during those lean student days.

Sometimes the president of the college would issue a special invitation to select students to dine at his home. This was a great honor and a much sought-after invitation. One day, I received one of those special invitations. I was astonished that he was even aware of my existence as I scurried like a little mouse from campus to newspaper office, from the McCall's where I ironed shirts, and back to campus again.

Oh dear! What was I to wear? I only had my three drab little day dresses and my thin old jacket. I owned absolutely nothing formal, and my everyday clothes were so shabby from constant washing and ironing that I couldn't imagine showing up at the gracious home of the college president in them.

The wonderful, generous girls of the Senior Hall came to my rescue. Rosemary, a petite little blonde cried, "I have a perfect blue frock that I think would look wonderful on you." And she rushed off to her room to get it.

Then Doris piped up. "What size shoe do you wear? I believe my navy pumps will fit those tiny feet of yours."

Then Mildred and Woody tossed in a jaunty little hat with a feather and a pair of soft, white kidskin gloves to finish the ensemble. Another girl, whose name I don't even remember, placed a lovely cashmere coat around my shoulders. Grateful tears sprang to my eyes as I rushed across campus to the president's house in my borrowed finery. The president hosted a grand party and then regaled us with readings from Shakespeare throughout the dinner.

Senior Hall - Eastern College of Education, Cheney Washington

Don and Ted Quit School

In the summer of 1938, Father was working for Mr. Mickey and my family was living on a farm he owned in the Lance Hills. Twelve year-old Ted got a job shocking oats at the Corley farm. He managed to finish work there in time to start school that fall.

The Lance Hill country is a series of rolling hills south of Cheney between Tyler and Sprague. There are several small lakes and outcroppings of rock that separate the area from the wheat fields to the west and north. It is a small but rich wheat-producing area.

My brother Don was in high school and busy with his classes. He had chosen to grow a field of potatoes for his agriculture project. He harvested them in the fall and sold the crop for the handsome sum of three hundred dollars. That was his first taste of profit from farming and he was excited about it.

Don had quickly mastered the big machinery used in the wheat fields. He was taking his turn plowing and harrowing in the big hills, getting ready for the fall seeding. He was interested in wheat farming. He saw it as an easier life than running a dairy operation. The steep hills had been a challenge to horse-drawn machinery, but with the new gas powered tractors, harrowing, seeding, weeding, and harvesting was much easier.

As young men, Don and Ted were interested in this new way of farming. Don knew that the unfamiliar equipment would be a challenge for Father. The boys helped all they could on weekends and after school.

Soon Don realized how much Father needed him in the field, and he decided to quit school.

As time went on, it became more and more difficult for me to spend time out on the wheat ranch with my family. Weekends were manageable, but getting to the ranch every night proved impossible. Earl was working at the creamery and going to college. Sometimes he could find time to drive me out to the Lance Hills place. But without a car of my own, I saw less and less of my family.

That first winter proved to be a challenge. Lots of snow fell in the Lance Hills, and bitter winds blew the snow into hard-packed drifts. Roads were often closed, leaving ranchers stranded for long periods of time. Father and the boys spent their winter days repairing machinery and tending to the livestock.

As the holiday season drew near, Mother and Edith got jobs plucking turkeys on a large turkey farm nearby. Picking the feathers off the turkey carcasses was a cold, miserable job. They slogged through snow for better than a mile to get to work. The work was hard on the fingers. Although the pay was good, they were glad when the holiday season was over.

In the spring Edith graduated from high school and in the fall started college. She and Ted were riding in on the school bus, but getting to the bus stop required a long hike out over several steep hills, through the snow and bitter cold wind. It was a challenge to get to the bus on time. When the fall semester ended, Edith decided that she didn't want to continue with college. She would rather stay at the ranch and help mother with the chickens and housework.

As the war was heating up, many young men chose to enlist in the service before being called up. That way they could choose the navy or air force rather than become foot soldiers in the army. It became difficult to find young men for hire to work in the fields. Ted was in high school that next winter, and again the heavy snows made walking to catch the school bus difficult. When spring came around, and the new crop was ready for seeding, Ted decided to quit school too and go to work with Father and Don in the wheat fields.

Don, Edith, Ernestine, and Ted
Comstock Park Spokane

Don McMillan

Edith McMillan
High School Graduation, 1939

Natatorium Park

I thought Earl was very sophisticated. He had done so many amazing things. I never dreamed of doing such things growing up on the poor little farm on the Green Meadow. He travelled all alone on the train to visit his cousins in Seattle. He was a good swimmer and was allowed to go swimming in Fish Lake with his friends. He could ice skate. He went fishing with his parents and had his own fishing gear. He was skillful with the boat. He had his own car and drove it to school. He had a quiet confidence about him that I admired very much.

We were both so busy we never even entertained the idea of dating other people. We had been together since junior high school. Both of us were working part-time and helping out at home, to say nothing of our busy student activities. Some summers we didn't see each other until Earl's August birthday when his mother would pack a picnic lunch, and we would all go to the lake.

One special Fourth of July, Earl's family had a big picnic at the Natatorium Park in Spokane. Natatorium Park began as a trolley park, one of many that sprang up across the country in the late 1890's. These parks were often owned by the trolley lines and were placed at the end of the tracks to give people a reason to ride.

The park had a baseball diamond and a swimming pool that was filled with heated water from the Spokane River. The pool was called The Natatorium after the Latin word for swimming pool. The park was known as Nat Park or The Nat by locals.

Nat Park featured a beautifully landscaped garden and picnic grounds, along with a lily pond and an elaborate outdoor fountain. It was located on the bank of the Spokane River. More and more attractions were added over the years to keep interest in the park alive. Top-name entertainers played at the park. Earl and I loved to dance to the big band music at the Dance Palace. All the great bands played there, including our favorites, Jimmy and Tommy Dorsey, Kay Kyser, and Benny Goodman.

Geyser Fountain at Natatorium Park, Spokane Washington

Nat Park had a famous merry-go-round. It was called the Looff Carousel and was built in 1909. The carousel sported fifty-four horses, a giraffe, a tiger and two chariots, all hand carved by the famous carousel carver, Charles Looff. It also had a brass ring dispenser that allowed the outside riders to grab a ring during each pass and then toss the ring at a clown with a hole for his mouth. If the rider was successful in capturing the brass ring, he won a free ride on the carousel.

That Independence Day, Earl's mother packed a huge picnic lunch. It was a perfect summer day, hot and clear with a little breeze blowing off the river. All his cousins came with their dates. We found a good spot on the picnic grounds and stayed all day and far into the night. Earl's dad even planned to go home to milk the cows and then come back to spend the evening.

There were so many things to do in the park. Earl loved a ride called the Chutes. The Shoot-the-Chutes ride was a contraption that carried boats up a ramp on a track and then released them back down the track ending in a tremendous splash in a small shallow lake.

The Chutes, Natatorium Park, Spokane Washington

We had fun chasing each other around in the bumper cars. He'd slam into me and make me squeal, and I'd go charging after him to exact my revenge.

Later, as evening approached and the lights of the park began to wink on, we rode the Ferris Wheel to watch the sunset. The wheel suddenly stopped with our gondola at the top, rocking back and forth. Earl put his arm around me, pretending to calm my fears, and then he kissed me so suddenly that the gondola rocked even harder. When our feet were back firmly on the ground, we rode the famous carousel with its happy calliope music filling the night air. The horses pranced round and round, and the boys stretched out to catch the gold ring for another spin. As darkness descended on the park, we spread out blankets on the grass and laid back to watch the dazzling fireworks exploding in the night sky.

Those were our carefree summer days, but Hitler was Chancellor of Germany and as the decade wore on, Germany's policy of aggression against its European neighbors made it clear that war was coming.

The Nazi threat in Europe was like a dark storm cloud gathering on the horizon. We listened to the radio and watched the newsreels at the Melodian. As each European nation fell to the Nazis, it seemed that the storm grew ever closer to home. The young men of our crowd all believed that soon the United States would be in it.

Hilton & McMillan families join in a 4th of July picnic at Comstock Park

Front Row: My cousin Royal Roberts, Earl, Ernestine, Earl's cousins Joe Franks & Renee Franks, Don's date, and Don McMillan

Back Row: Earl's mother Lura Hilton, Ted McMillan, my mother Myrtle McMillan, Ted's future wife Loraine, Edith McMillan, and my father Ernest McMillan

The Twitching Curtain

The winter quarter of 1940-41 Mr. and Mrs. Mickey asked my sister Edith and me to stay in their house and watch over their old gray cat, the Commodore. They were spending the winter in California. The house was new and had a warm furnace and a wonderful modern kitchen. Best of all, it was only a few blocks from campus. Edith and I were acquainted with everyone in the neighborhood. The strain of juggling my runaround life ended. We not only had a roof over our heads, we were in the very lap of luxury.

Earl was a busy college student as well. He continued to work at the Cheney Creamery part-time. He came to the Mickey house often on Friday or Saturday night to take me out. Earl's shiny red truck was quite distinctive, and everyone in town knew both of us. I was still playing fiddle in my little dance band, and we were often away at country dances until the wee hours of the morning.

Earl was always very careful of my reputation. He parked right in front of the house, knocked loudly, and waited under the porch light to be admitted. He gave the nosey neighbors plenty of time to identify him. He never stayed late at night. We were very well aware of the curtains twitching as certain neighbors monitored Earl's comings and goings. We were two single girls living alone in a big house. It was inevitable that Earl and I would become the target of nasty gossip.

One morning when I arrived at class, I was handed a request to report to the Dean of Women Students' office immediately. I couldn't imagine why she wanted to see me, but I soon found out. The dean was known to be a rather prudish, old-fashioned lady, and I did not know her well. As soon as I stepped into her office, without any preliminary pleasantries whatsoever, she lit in to me.

"Miss McMillan, you know better than that!" she said, leaning back in her chair and giving me a stern look." It has come to my attention that you are living in an unacceptable situation. No student is allowed to live off campus without a proper chaperone. I will have to suspend you from school until this is cleared up."

I was stunned. I was so close to graduation. I tried to explain the circumstances to her, but she wouldn't listen, waving me away and rustling the papers on her desk in dismissal. I couldn't argue with her. I just meekly said I would take care of it and left the room. I had never heard of the chaperone requirement. I knew lots of co-eds living off campus, either alone or with other girls. I could have pointed that out to the dean, but I didn't want anyone else to get in trouble. I returned to class.

I was beginning to get angry. The dean had never remarked on my living situation when I had wandered from house to house looking for a bed to sleep in, practically homeless, for most of my college career. As soon as class was over, I went in search of Earl. I was very upset that someone thought something improper was going on at the Mickey house. Some nasty-minded busybody had talked to the dean.

I needed to talk with Earl, my Incredible Man. Calm and quiet as always, Earl drove me out to see my parents. The four of us talked it over. Mother sat right down and wrote a letter to the dean, pointing out that I was 21 years old, living with my sister and providing a service for a fine Cheney family. She mentioned that Earl was a trustworthy young man from a good family.

I held my breath for a week or two, but I heard nothing more from the dean. Mother's letter had explained the situation satisfactorily. Or perhaps the dean had thought better of her actions. Earl continued to come to pick me up in his red truck. I believe he even occasionally winked at the twitching curtain in the house next door.

Earl on Campus

Ernestine on Campus

Love in Uncertain Times

It was during our years together in college that Earl and I found our close friendship blossoming into true love. Both of us were very busy. Earl continued to work for Milton Hunt at the Creamery in the morning before class. I was busy too, involved in my college work, editing the school paper, working as a newspaper correspondent for the Spokane Chronicle and finishing my final year at college. We spent lunchtimes and study times together whenever we could. If we were really lucky and had a little break, we loved going out for a ride in the country, singing songs as we drove around the wheat hills beyond the college campus.

In September of 1940, Congress had passed the Selective Training and Service Act. This law required all men between the ages of 21 and 35 to register with local draft boards. Earl realized that the United States would soon be in the war. He would be eligible for the draft as soon as he reached his 21st birthday. He dreaded the idea of going to war.

Our love for each other was maturing, and we were both concerned about the future. During the time we spent together we tried to put our worries aside. Earl was hoping to finish college. He liked his studies in animal husbandry and was anxious to try out his ideas for cattle breeding. He also excelled in mathematics and sometimes thought about becoming a math teacher. We both knew that in his heart he wanted to be a rancher.

Earl learned that exemptions were granted for certain occupation like miners, farmers, mariners and railway workers. Finally, he sat down for a serious talk with his dad, asking to go in with him on the ranch. His dad, although sympathetic and understanding, told Earl that he preferred him go out on his own for awhile. He wanted him to experience working for someone else, then if he was still interested, his dad would take him on.

As the pressure of war heated up, Earl reluctantly gave up his hopes of remaining on the ranch with his dad. He began to look for a job where he could manage his own affairs. That fall semester he was sending out resumes with letters of recommendation, hoping to find work beyond school.

Earl invited me to spend Thanksgiving Day with his family. He was an only child and was always pleased to have company. Over the years I had spent lots of time with his family. Two cousins with their dates joined us for dinner. His mother was a wonderful cook. The Thanksgiving dinner was delicious and his dad carved the turkey at the table.

After dinner Earl and I went for a walk. The fall afternoon was balmy, the sky blue and cloudless. He wanted to show me the big meadows of the Rocky Pine Ranch and the tall basalt bluffs that surrounded them. Brown cattails beside a small pond rustled in the breeze. We walked to the top of a bluff and scanned the land that now lay dormant, ready for its winter sleep.

Here, spread before us, was a meadowland, big and rich, its autumn grasses swaying with the wind. My memories of the Green Meadow of my childhood seemed tiny by comparison, yet thoughts of that loss still tugged at my heart. I understood now how much Earl loved this place. I understood his wish to stay here on this land.

We walked down from the bluff into the meadow itself. There beside a little pond we found a bunch of fallen cattails. Dried by the summer sun, they made a perfect couch. We sat down upon them and talked about the land and the future.

"Someday I want to build a house for us here on the ranch," Earl said wistfully, taking a little notebook from his shirt pocket. He began to draw a picture of the kind of house he would build. I imagined a pretty Cape Cod, but Earl said no. Our house would have to be modern and spacious, with lots of rooms.

The big meadows of the Rocky Pine Ranch

"For all the kids, you know." he said, giving me a nudge and a wink. "How about two fireplaces?" he asked with a grin. "With a rug for Ole Baldy and bookshelves filled with lots of books for winter reading." He looked at me with a question in his eyes.

Then I asked, "what if you have to go away and leave all this?"

"Little brown eyes," he said to me. "Let's not worry now. I may have to go away. But I love you and I will always come back."

That day out in the meadow we planned our dream house. Like other young couples faced with war, we tried to put our worries aside. Earl continued to look for a job and I couldn't wait to get started on my teaching career.

Earl & Ernestine in the meadow at Rocky Pine Ranch

Graduation Day

Finally, in the spring of 1941, it was Gradation Day. I had completed four years of college in three. The sky was clear, and the June sun was already warm when I met Clare in the Commuter Students room. We put on our caps and gowns. Our faithful friend and Camp Fire Guardian, Lulu Cutting was already there, waiting to help us get ready for the big day. She carefully adjusted our caps to the proper angle.

"There you are," she said as she stood back to take a look at us. "I am so very proud of you both!"

She gave us a quick hug, careful not to knock off our caps. She walked with us out onto the campus lawn. There she took our picture. Clare and I stood in the shade of the Chinese Elm beside the library, hesitating to join the long twisting chain of cap and gown clad students that was forming on the lawn outside the auditorium. Our school days were over. Our adult lives were about to begin.

Suddenly a doubt crept in to stand beside us as we stood in the shade of the red brick building. Had it been enough? In a few minutes we would be handed our teaching certificates and our college degrees. Would we know what to do come September when we had to open that door and face our own classrooms full of students? Would we suddenly be transformed into that amazing beast, "The Teacher"?

In the gathering heat of the June morning, we looked at each other, reading each other's minds, as we so often did. Then we gathered our gowns around us. Our hearts and minds commanded and our feet responded. We left the shelter of the library and found ourselves striding across the dandelion-sprinkled lawn to join our graduating class.

Ernestine and Clare, College Graduation 1941

Clare's mother and father were in the audience. My parents had not come. Mr. Mickey had chosen that day to brand cattle, and of course, work always came first with Father. He would never have suggested that branding could wait so he could watch his eldest child graduate from college. I wished that someone had brought Mother. I looked around desperately hoping that someone from my family would be there for my big day.

It was difficult for Mother, I rationalized. Perhaps she had nothing appropriate to wear. But surely my sister, or one of my brothers could have brought her. Why weren't they there at least? I had worked so hard for this day. Perhaps I was the only one who considered it a special day.

Just then, I saw Earl striding across the campus toward me. He walked with such an easy, loose-jointed grace. Just seeing him lifted my heart.

Happiness flowed through me. This day was mine, family or no. And here, was my best friend coming to share it with me. He took my hand and placed a delicate gold watch around my wrist and handed me a red rose. It was suddenly a very lovely, extra special day.

The march into Showalter Hall was long and hot. Music resonated in the big old auditorium. It was a fine moment when our names were read. I graduated summa cum laude, and tucked inside my diploma was my teaching certificate. All the hardship and difficulty, all the missed meals and shabby clothes were behind me. I had set my sights on my goal so long ago and here I was, holding it in my very own hand, a teaching certificate.

A few days after graduation, Earl came to say goodbye. He had talked it over with his parents and had made up his mind to go to Seattle in search of a job. It was hard to see him go. He wanted to stay and work with his dad on the ranch. But he didn't have much choice. We took one last long drive out over the wheat hills, before we joined his parents at the train station to send him on his way. He had cousins and friends in Seattle. I knew he would be alright, but I would miss him so very much.

FORTY-NINTH ANNUAL

COMMENCEMENT

Eastern Washington College of Education

at

Cheney, Washington

Ernestine J. McMillan

JUNE TWELFTH
1941

Ernestine's College Graduation Announcement

Home Again

I put aside any thoughts of the next step in my life. I knew I would need to secure a teaching position. But that could wait a little bit longer. For now I was going home to rest. I wanted to spend this summer with my family. Things had turned for the better for Mother and Father. With the steady support from Mr. Mickey, Father had moved ahead and rented a place on Granite Lake Road. It was a nice house with electricity, a bathroom and plenty of bedrooms. Father was wheat farming on his own and doing well. Mother still had her chickens and a big garden.

It had been a long time since we had all been together. What a pleasure it was to go to sleep in the peace and quiet of the countryside in a bed of my own. Again, birds woke me in the morning, singing in the trees outside my window. Mother let me sleep and wake on my own time. She knew I was exhausted and needed time to rest.

As I lay in bed, just waking up, I often heard my brothers playing their guitars and singing before they went out to the field. Their voices were no longer the piping of little boys, but the rich deep tones of young men. I had been so busy over the past three years, that I hadn't realized how they'd grown. Suddenly, standing there, on the brink of my new life, my family seemed all the more precious to me. It was good to be home.

As a graduation gift for me and Clare, Mrs. Findley wanted to take us to visit the world's fair in San Francisco. We had seen newsreels about the Golden Gate International Exposition that had been held in 1939 and 1940 at Treasure Island. The world's fair celebrated the city's two new bridges; the Oakland Bay Bridge dedicated in 1936, and the mighty Golden Gate Bridge finished in 1937.

Golden Gate International Exposition,Treasure Island, 1939

I especially wanted to see the Yaquina Bay Bridge in Newport, Oregon. I had studied the work of its builder, Conde B. McCollough, in my art classes in college. He had designed and built several beautiful bridges along the Oregon coast and I was anxious to see them. Mrs. Findley was planning to drive down the west coast highway. Clare and I poured over the maps. We studied the California missions and the many bridges along the coast.

Mrs. Findley took us shopping and bought us each a dress to wear on the trip. When Father heard about that, he stepped in and put a stop to the whole enterprise. I supposed he felt humiliated at not having done anything special for my graduation. Or perhaps he felt that the Findley family was going overboard. Mother tried to explain Father's reasons. Whatever they may have been, he forbade me to go, and I was heartbroken.

I found it very difficult to forgive him. I secretly mourned over it for a long time. The Findleys seemed to understand, but Clare and I didn't.

Clare and I cried together. In fact, I cried buckets over the injustice of it all.

Even so, I was happy to be home with my family. I spent the early morning hours down in the big garden that Mother had planted just below the house. Just like my childhood days on the Green meadow, I was out early on dewy mornings, hoeing weeds in the corn patch. Slowly the mental fatigue left me, and each day I found renewed happiness with my family.

Mother never called me in the morning, letting me sleep as long as I liked. I spent my days just being lazy, enjoying the quiet of the countryside and the happiness of being home. Once again I wandered in the fields, stopping to lie on my back in the tall grass and let the wind whisper over me. I had a sense of timelessness just watching the clouds of summer slip silently across the sky. The sweet serenity of that summer was my last backward glance at my childhood.

It was early July when a letter came from the Placement Office telling me that they had arranged an appointment for me with the Spangle School Board. Although I had hoped for something in Western Washington so I could be near Earl, I was delighted at the prospect of teaching in Spangle, a community only a few miles away from home.

The school board members were men who had danced to my fiddle, and I felt comfortable with them. Spangle was a country town, where I would feel at home. I signed the contract for the school year and soon began getting my things ready to move to Spangle.

I was informed that there was an opening for me to stay in the Gruenwald home not far from the schoolhouse. I went to Spangle to have a look. I found a homey house with a smiling Mrs. Gruenwald, who showed me around. There was a spacious room upstairs, just waiting for a tenant. It had a window that looked southward out across the fields of grain. The bed had a homemade quilt for a coverlet. There was a chest of drawers, a cherry wood desk, a mirror and a rocking chair. There was a big closet and a little stove to take the chill off on a winter morning. I would share the bathroom on the landing on the stairs. I liked it all very much and rented it on the spot.

My lack of a wardrobe was again a problem. I hadn't minded wandering about the farm in my shabby old dresses and broken down shoes, but suddenly I was a professional woman. I was quite penniless until my job actually began and I received a paycheck. I had spent what little money I had on graduation gifts for my friends. Now, the real world crowded back on me and I began to worry.

As always, Mother came to the rescue. By selling a few of her hens, she gave me enough money to buy material for three new dresses that she helped me sew. A navy blue rayon shirtwaist with white trim, a nice sage green plaid with pleated skirt and a soft brown rayon with long sleeves and a circle skirt completed my wardrobe. I still had my two skirts and white blouses that I often wore with bright scarves and ties. A new pair of shoes and my wardrobe was complete.

The day before I was to go to Spangle, Mother gave my hair a trim. I was reminded of the day, back at our home on the Green Meadow, when Mother and Cecil had first chopped off my sun-bleached curls. I had been a toddler then; now I was a grown woman preparing to make my own way in the world.

I Pay a Debt

I was enjoying carefree days with my family on the wheat farm on Granite Lake Road, recovering from the intense years of study. As I reflected upon those days spent on campus, I was reminded of the kindness of the McCall family. They had taken me into their home, giving me a place to stay that enabled me to work on the Spokane Chronicle.

After I had been at home for a few weeks, I went to visit the McCall family. I wanted to thank Mrs. McCall for her generosity through the years. Without her assistance, I might not have reached my goal. I wanted to do something for her that would show my deep gratitude for the many times she had provided a warm bed and a place to study.

Mrs. McCall was intensely interested in the Coulee Dam project. The waters of the Columbia were beginning to back up in the river. Many little towns north of the dam would soon to be inundated by the rising waters. The little town of Peach on a northern stretch of the Columbia River was about to be lost. Houses were being torn down and the debris taken away.

Peach was the town where Mrs. McCall was born. She was following the stories in the paper as one by one the towns disappeared under the rising water. She often said that she would like to go see her former home once more before it too was inundated. So I made a suggestion. I would be glad to drive her to see Peach before it was lost forever.

Marie McCall, the sister nearest my age, was to be married in August and was busy with her wedding plans. I could see that she too needed a break. I had a road map in my car and that day we began to make plans to take Mrs. McCall back to the place where she was born.

Mrs. McCall had not had an easy life. When her youngest child was only two weeks old, her husband passed away, leaving her with five children to care for. Mrs. McCall's brothers and sisters helped her by each taking a child for the summer, giving her time to take on extra work or have some time for herself.

She hadn't been home to Peach in many years, and she was eager to visit her family and see her hometown before it was gone. She had never owned a car and seldom was spared time away from her endless work as she raised her family. A trip would be a welcome change for her. Marie and her mother wrote to family members, and in a few days we had an itinerary.

We set off early one morning to visit with her family in Creston, the area of Lincoln County on the Columbia Plateau that produces large quantities of wheat. First we stopped to see her brother Carl and his family. It was mid-July and harvest time. Kenny McCall, her only son, was there working for his Uncle Carl. Harvest was in full swing. Teams of horses pulled the combines through the wheat fields, as the golden kernels poured into the busy sack-sewers' hands.

Feeding a full harvest crew was a big job. The women began their work even as the men were leaving for the field and the breakfast dishes were cleared away. Kenny had stayed behind that day to help with the heavy work of the kitchen, the lifting and carrying. The women chattered and laughed as they began the preparation of a harvest dinner. The men would come in hungry and hot. They would spend an hour eating and resting away from the hottest part of the day and then return to the field for several more hours of hard work.

All the women in the house helped prepare the massive meal. Heat from the big woodstove was like a furnace in the farmhouse kitchen. Sweat poured down the women's faces as they worked. There were heaping platters of fried chicken, bowls of potatoes and gravy, and piles of fresh vegetables from the garden to prepare for the table. Cakes and pies sat cooling on the windowsill, ready to serve the crew. The extra help from us visitors was welcome. We enjoyed a lively visit as we worked. Mrs. McCall was beaming with happiness when she sat down with her brother and his family to enjoy the harvest meal. Everyone talked of olden times.

At the end of the day's work, the family again lingered at the supper table, laughing over tales told of long ago days. We sat until the heat of the day eased, hoping for a night wind to cool the sleeping hours. In the morning we rose with the sun that was soon blazing in the heat of the summer day.

The next day the family made a visit to the old cemetery located in the hamlet of Egypt, not far from the farm. There we saw the small church and the old schoolhouse where Mrs. McCall had gone to school. She lingered over the grave of her husband. It was a fine visit, and after a few days, we set off to find our next destination, the little town of Peach, farther north up the Columbia River. We rose at sunup and began our journey to avoid the sweltering heat that would fill the car as the sun rose higher.

We drove by the towering structure of the Grand Coulee Dam to have a look at the great activity that surrounded the area where it was being built. Continuing on our journey, we drove north beside the river until we found what was left of Peach.

As the water continued to rise, most of the buildings had been removed. Few structures remained. The concrete streets were being torn up by big tractors that scooped up the debris. All that was left of the houses were broken chunks of concrete from the foundations scattered along the shore of the river. Mrs. McCall was able to locate what remained of some of the old buildings that she remembered from her childhood.

Walking along the Columbia River, we came to a spot that Mrs. McCall believed was the site where she was born. Nothing remained of the house or the orchard that she remembered so well. She stood at the spot she believed the house once stood. We had a little box camera with us and Marie took her picture standing there squinting into the sun. As she wandered along the sandy shore of the river, she found a silver spoon and carried it away in her pocket.

We now retraced our steps back down along the Columbia River, going through the canyons of the Grand Coulee on our way to the city of Pasco. We drove through the orchards of Wenatchee where apple trees were loaded with ripening fruit. The July day was very hot, and we were glad when we arrived at twilight at the home of her daughter, Della.

We spent several comfortable days there visiting with her family. We all helped pick cherries and corn and helped with the canning. Mrs. McCall's oldest daughter, Georgia and her young son, Billy, were also visiting there and rode back home to Cheney with us.

We were glad to be back home. Mrs. McCall had enjoyed the trip although it was bittersweet to see her childhood home in ruins. It was a gift I was glad I could give to the woman who had been so kind to me.

Ernestine and Marie McCall

I Go to Teach in Spangle

When the time came to pack up my things to go to Spangle, I put them in boxes. I didn't own a suitcase. When everything was loaded into our car, Father and Mother drove me to Spangle, about thirty miles away. I would be staying at the home of the Grunewalds, where I was to live in an upstairs room next to the school librarian. We arrived on a warm August evening, exchanged a brief goodbye, and Mother and Father drove away.

I felt like an abandoned child as my parents' car disappeared down the hill and out of sight. It was one of those uncertain moments in my life when I suddenly felt completely alone. Here was the great moment I had worked so long and hard for, and instead of triumphant, I felt very lonely. I recovered as best I could and went upstairs to put away my things.

Soon my next door roommate, Madelyn Carroll, arrived, and we hit it off immediately. We each had our own bedroom upstairs with plenty of closet space. Madelyn was 12 years older. As the school librarian and English teacher in Spangle for many years, she was a fixture in the community. She was warm and friendly, and would be a great help to me. I soon learned that I could turn to her for advice. I was very lucky to have her nearby.

That night Madelyn and I visited with each other, calling back and forth from our rooms as we hung up our clothes and arranged our things. We were soon laughing and chatting away like old friends. She told me about our host, John Grunewald, in whose house we were to spend the coming school year.

Mr. Grunewald was the chairman of the school board. He operated one of the huge grain elevators beside the railroad tracks below his house at the north end of town. Madelyn also pointed out the school house, just a couple of blocks away. It sat on the hillside with a span of wide windows all along its eastern side. The next day I would go there to explore the school and begin to arrange my own classroom.

Our landlady, Mrs. Elizabeth Grunewald, who preferred to be called Lizzie, was a charming, industrious lady. I liked here immediately. A member of one of the older pioneer families in town, she was a fine house mother. She provided wholesome meals and clean, pleasant rooms. Their son and his family lived right next door. We would all share the same clothesline that ran between the two houses.

Their little 5 year-old grandson who lived next door often came over to play with us in the evening before he went to bed. Since there was no kindergarten in the Spangle school, he had to wait another year to go to school. It was nice to have a lively youngster around.

We scarcely saw Mr. Grunewald. The September days were still quite warm, and the final stage of the fall harvest was taking place. Trucks loaded with wheat were driven down out of the fields to the warehouses that stood near the railroad tracks, just a few city blocks below the Grunewald house. Mr. Grunewald was always up by dawn and off to the grain warehouses, long before Madelyn and I got out of bed.

It was the smell of coffee from the kitchen wafting up the staircase that roused us from our beds. It was time for us to face the day. Madelyn had lived in this house and taught in Spangle for a dozen years. Her idea of breakfast was two chocolate chip cookies and a cup of coffee to dunk them in. I longed for oatmeal or a scrambled egg. But I politely followed Madelyn's lead and ate my two cookies with a cup of cocoa. Later on, I bought a hot plate and took it to school where I made my own oatmeal.

The largest meal of the day was dinner at noon, and I was right at home as Madelyn and I shared it with John and Lizzie. Often, we were joined by their two grown sons who worked on their wheat ranches nearby. An assortment of relatives often dropped in to share the dinner.

The Grunewalds and Lizzie's family, the Hengens, were among the pioneers who had come to the Palouse country and settled in Spangle during the Oregon Trail years. Wonderful stories flowed back and forth when the families came together at those dinners. This was a fine way for me to get acquainted with folks in the neighborhood. It was at that large family table that I came to know the families whose children I would teach.

Spangle Elementary Teachers
Ernestine 3rd & 4th grade, Irma Mae 1st & 2nd, Kathryn 5th & 6th, and Madelyn librarian and my roommate

My Own Classroom

It was the first day of school at Spangle Elementary. I went to school early, ready to face that important day. Our landlady picked lovely bouquets of asters from her garden for us to take to our classrooms. It was a homey touch to mark the first day of school. The colorful flowers gave warmth to the bare room that would soon come alive with fifteen active third and fourth grade boys and girls. Reminded of my own first day of school, so many years ago, I had imagined that a flood of anxiety might come over me, but instead I felt calm.

I had done my student teaching at the college elementary school in Cheney with the fourth grade, so I felt comfortable with the 9 and 10 year-olds who would soon invade my classroom. When the school buses pulled up out front of the school and the chattering children rushed into the classrooms, I was ready. Years of preparation were behind me; now it was time to see if I could do the job.

Madelyn had agreed to stop by my classroom that morning to introduce the children. I was grateful for her presence. She knew every child. She called their names and teased them, one by one, as she measured each of them by her shoulder to see how much they had grown over the summer. This amused the children. As for me, I realized how lucky I was to learn from Madelyn, who had such an easy way with children.

The children had come into the classroom quickly, knowing which friend they wished to sit beside. When the bell rang I went to the piano, struck a few cords, then turned to my pupils and asked them what song they would like to sing. Hands went up quickly. With a little debate, the favorite soon proved to be *"America the Beautiful."* They all stood and sang loudly. Then somebody suggested *"Jimmy Crack Corn"* followed by *"Three Blind Mice."* They sang confidently, their little voices mingling together.

Someone suggested that we salute the flag, and when that was over, they settled down in their seats and looked at me expectantly. I asked the fourth graders to take out their arithmetic books and go to work on some simple problems. The third graders and I went to the front of the room where I had arranged several new books around a table. There we sat and read a story together.

My classroom at Spangle Elementary School

Time passed quickly, and before we knew it, it was time for lunch. The lunchroom was in the high school building next door. The children from the country went off to join the rest of their schoolmates in the cafeteria. The city children walked home for lunch. For most of those children, this meant a big dinner at the table with their whole family. The first hour after lunch was sometimes difficult because I was faced with sleepy children after the heavy meal.

The children were reading well and could master arithmetic. Most were being raised in comfortable homes with loving, helpful parents.

They were well mannered and eager to learn. Spangle was an affluent community with a fine school, well supplied with books and learning materials. I was even given an National Youth Administration aid. She was a high school senior who came to my classroom to help with recordkeeping.

The National Youth Administration was a New Deal agency operated from 1935 to 1943 as part of the WPA. High school and college youth were enlisted for work-study projects at their schools. Unlike the Civil Conservation Corps, the NYA employed young women.

I still recall the names of every one of those students in my class at Spangle. The boys were Phil, Eddy, Roland, Ronnie, Kenny, Dallas, Irwin, Larry, Bobby and Aaron. The girls were Shirley, Violet, Wanda, Donna and Barbara. I loved all the children and went eagerly to my classroom every morning.

When school was out for the day, I would walk to the post office in downtown Spangle. The scorching heat of summer had passed, and the September weather was perfect. After a busy day in the classroom, the fresh air and hum of bees in the purple thistles along the sidewalk was relaxing.

Ladies would come out onto their porches and call to me as I strolled along."Stop by on your way back and have a cup of coffee." It felt like home, hearing those friendly folks as I walked along. Those little visits over back fences and on front porches helped me to feel like a part of the community.

My daily walk to the post office was often rewarded with a letter from Earl. If there was a letter postmarked Seattle in my box, my day was complete. Not much was said in those letters, but Earl wrote almost daily, and I could read between the lines. He had good reason to keep his letters short. His days were long at Doran's Machine Shop, where he had found work. The job provided him with an income as well as a draft deferment because the machine shop provided parts for the big warships being built in the shipyards of Bremerton.

I was teaching on the first Teachers' Contract that the State Legislature had mandated with a beginning salary of $100 dollars a month. I counted my money carefully. My room and board at Grunewald's was $25 a month. I sent my Mother $25 every month. She needed and deserved it. That left me with $50, some of it I would spend, some of it went into my bank account. I felt like a millionaire.

My class at Spangle Elementary School

Front Row: Ronnie Hart, Dallas Graham, Larry Knuth, Irwin Johnson.

Middle Row: Donna Owes, Violet Brown, Wanda Brash, Shirley Sires, Barbara Green.

Back Row: Aaron Brash, Kenny Baird, Eddy Hengen, Phil Hall, Bobby Green, Ernestine McMillan (Teacher), Ronald Suksdorf.

The Boy Who Wouldn't Read

One cold, snowy morning I went to school early to make sure that the classroom would be warm when the children arrived. As I came up to the front steps, there was a little boy standing at the door. He was dancing about from one foot to the other trying to keep warm in the freezing cold morning air. It was Aaron, a boy in my third grade class. He wore no jacket and was stomping his feet and clapping his hands.

"Aaron!" I said. "What are you doing out here on the porch so early?"

"I rode in with my dad," he said. "I was waiting for you." His blue eyes sparkling, he kept jumping up and down in the cold. Then he looked up at me with his eager smile.

"Teach," he said. "You have the key!"

I hustled him into the room, brushed the snow from his hair and shoulders, and sat him down by the nearest heater under the eastern window. His lips were blue with cold. He was the youngest in his family. His father worked hard to provide for his children. However, times were tough, and I realized that Aaron often came to school hungry. That morning I shared the oatmeal and toast that I prepared on my hotplate.

Aaron's older sister, the oldest child in my classroom, was 12 year-old Wanda. She was already physically mature, but still in the fourth grade. She was a plodding learner, and I knew she tried hard. Among other difficulties, she was the oldest child in a motherless home. She had the responsibility of caring for their home and preparing supper after school. It had to be on the table when their father got home from work. That left very little time for schoolwork. Wanda was so burdened with cares that she often came to school too exhausted to learn.

It was Aaron, however, who was my greatest challenge. He was a cute little fellow, bright and quick, but somehow he had become convinced that he was too dumb to learn. "So why try?" he told me with a shrug of his skinny shoulders. His greatest ambition was to be like his older brother who was a sixth grader. The brother took great pride in brawling and cursing on the playfield. The children in that family had few advantages but they seemed bright enough.

That morning when Aaron looked at me with his bright eyes and said, "Teach, you have the key," I realized that he really believed in me. Those words from that little boy have never left my mind. I often think of him, so confident that the teacher would always be there with the key. The weight of his boyish confidence that cold morning has remained with me. As a teacher I felt so responsible for him and for the other children that filled my classroom. Every child expects that the teacher has the key, not only to unlock the school door, but also the key to learning.

After that, on many of those wintery mornings, I would find Aaron on the porch steps when I came to school. He was a stubborn boy who was convinced that he would never be able to read. His excuse was that a previous teacher had told him that he was too dumb. However, I knew he was bright enough to know that not being able to read was something to be ashamed of. It was no wonder that he had become belligerent and approached the world in a sassy fashion to cover up for what was lacking. It was obvious that he was undernourished and hungry.

I decided to test him. I told him that he could share a cup of cocoa with me if he would help me prepare it. That meant that he would need to read the instructions on the package in order to make it. Hungry and eager to please me, he grunted, groaned and stammered as we read through the first line on the package. Looking at me out of the corner of his eye, he struggled to sound out the words. I pointed out a word or two. I was quite sure that he could read if he tried hard.

He did his best, and with some coaching, he got through the first sentence. I gave him a pat on the back, and handed him a spoon to put the cocoa into his cup. The water in the pan on the hot plate was ready, and he stood back while I poured it over the cocoa. Aaron kept his eyes on every movement I made. And when we sat down together for our breakfast, I knew I had him hooked.

All that winter we cooked our breakfast together, with Aaron sounding out the words. The sparkle in his eyes told me what was going on in his head. The pushing and shoving on the playground gradually stopped. With a warm breakfast in his belly, Aaron's attention turned to the world around him. He sat quietly as his classmates read, and finally one day he raised his hand and volunteered to stand and read aloud.

We had many conversations those winter mornings, just the two of us, over warm oatmeal and cocoa. His self confidence began to grow as he learned to read. It was soon clear that he knew more than he pretended to know; he was as bright as I suspected. He was tight-lipped and sullen about the troubles at home. Perhaps he wanted to forget all that for a small span of time while he was with me. With a little kindness, patience, and attention, the boy was blossoming.

Every Friday morning, I sent the fourth graders to the blackboard for a contest in arithmetic. It was a relay. The class chose sides, and I would put a problem on the board. The student with the first hand up would go to the board and write the answer. Hands would fly into the air when I began with simple problems. Fewer hands went up as the problem became more difficult. The side that solved the most problems would win.

One day I watched Aaron. He was working in the third grade arithmetic book and not very enthusiastic about it. When the fourth graders had arithmetic races, I saw Aaron squirming in his seat, his eyes sparkling, his mouth working silently, as he watched the fourth graders run to the board. I kept my eye on him.

The following week, when the fourth graders were having a relay, I watched Aaron. He was mouthing answers to himself. I quickly turned away from a problem I had just placed on the board and called him up. He looked at me, and when I nodded, he grabbed the chalk and wrote the correct answer on the board.

A shout went up from the fourth graders. Amazed that ornery little

Aaron knew the answer to their problem, they laughed and clapped. Aaron, unaccustomed to any appreciation, hung his head, but with shiny eyes he returned to his seat.

Aaron Brash

From that moment on, Aaron had won the respect of his peers. The fourth graders now saw Aaron as a different boy. They welcomed him to play the arithmetic game with them. They treated him more kindly and he was often included in their games. That day, Aaron had won a great victory for himself.

Aaron had often spoken of his desire to have a dog of his own. I knew that I could not answer that wish. Each day he carefully read the directions and fed the goldfish I kept on my desk. He had proven to me that he could read the package of fish food needed to feed the fish. One day I gave him a pair of goldfish of his own. He chose not to take them home, but proudly took care of them at school. He fed them daily and kept their bowl clean. He was happy to have something that was his alone. Before the year was over, Aaron was reading with his class and ready to go on to fourth grade.

Thanksgiving and the Whistling Boys

It didn't take many weeks for me to find out that the boys and girls in my classroom had good music skills. No doubt some of them had come from homes where music was sung and played. Most homes that had electricity also had a radio. Radios were also beginning to be standard equipment in the new car models. Musical variety shows were broadcast live almost every night.

We always started our day with a song. The children had their favorites. I had to be on my toes to keep ahead of them, to come up with new songs that they would quickly learn to sing. They would sit quietly in their seats and listen as I played the piano.

As we became more accustomed to each other, they all began to feel free to be themselves; I often heard them humming and singing as they went about their activities. I even heard some of the boys whistling. This gave me a thought.

One morning when the bell rang and everyone sat in their seats waiting for me to go to the piano, I turned to them and said, "This morning, when I play the song, I want you to stand up and, instead of singing, hum or try whistling the song. Does that sound like fun?"

There was some giggling and a few laughs. Then they settled down and, looking around at each other, they readily agreed. What transpired was interesting. Most of the children whistled. All the boys and some of the girls could whistle a tune. They loved music, no matter how it was made.

146

That morning, a new kind of music began in my classroom. The children were excited about it. Some would sing, some would just hum, and all of the boys whistled. It sounded wonderful, like a room full of canaries.

I found that the fourth grade boys were taking whistling very seriously. They listened carefully to the music as I played. They prided themselves on staying in tune. The boys monitored each other and were stern with anyone who might let out a giggle or stop in the middle of a tune. They soon found their favorite songs and asked for them eagerly when I went to the piano in the morning.

It wasn't long before five of the fourth grade boys, Philip, Eddy, Roland, Kenneth, and Ronald, formed a fine group of whistlers. They were quite serious and sounded lovely together. I put the girls in one group and the whistlers in another. Then we tried our favorite songs. That was good. Then I merged the whistlers with the singers. It all worked. Now we had a new kind of music.

Thanksgiving vacation was coming, and an all school holiday program was planned before the holiday break. I asked my children if they would like to perform in the program and sing and whistle. I could tell by their enthusiasm that they were all for it.

Their parents, having heard of our experiment, came to the program. I was nervous about the performance, but I knew that the children were enthusiastic, and that was all that mattered. While we waited back stage for our turn, I wondered what I had been thinking to try this. What would happen if just one of them started to giggle? We had practiced a lot, and sometimes things would just collapse and everyone would laugh. I knew that the children enjoyed the whistling and that they intended to do their best. But what if it all went horribly wrong?

When everyone was lined up backstage, I gave them a thumbs up and left to take a seat in the audience. As I crept away, I heard Phil, the tallest and best whistler. He was giving the boys a good talking to.

"Don't nobody laugh or I'll kill you myself!" he hissed. I took my seat out front and left my group in the capable fists of young Phil.

When the curtain came up, my boys whistled their song. The audience clapped and clapped. The boys whistled an encore. More applause.

Nobody laughed. The boys were a real hit. After that they were often asked to whistle in other programs, even a few times around town. They were so proud of themselves. And I was proud of them too. We all went off to our Thanksgiving holidays on a high note.

Earl had invited me to spend my long holiday weekend with him in Seattle. I had never ridden a bus across the country before, so it was a big adventure for me when I boarded the Greyhound and began the journey of 280 miles. I'd never been so far from home. I arrived in the dark in Earl's dream city. He met me at the bus station with a big hug and kiss. He was so anxious to show me the sights of the city.

When we stepped out onto the street we were instantly enveloped in dense fog. It was so thick that you couldn't even see the streetlights until you stood directly under them. The beautiful city that Earl was so eager to show me was nothing but a gray blur.

Earl had been living alone in a small apartment on Queen Ann Hill. But he had just purchased a used Ford and gone to live in a boarding house in West Seattle. I stayed with his cousins in West Seattle where we spent Thanksgiving Day. We had a wonderful time. Earl showed me where he worked down on the waterfront. The next day we went to Fauntleroy Park near where Earl had lived as a child. The fog was so thick, we couldn't see the ships, but we could hear the big blast of the whistle when the ships came into port. Earl told me how he was making those whistles in Doran's Shop.

We walked along the beach and found a place where we ate fish and chips. In the magic of that foggy day, Earl told me that when his salary reached eighty cents an hour, we would get married. We went downtown and picked out our engagement and wedding rings. Earl said he would have them paid for by spring.

The fog didn't lift until the very last afternoon when I was ready to leave for home. Then, for the first time, I saw Seattle with magnificent Mount Rainier gleaming in the background. I fell in love all over again, with the city, the mountain, and my Incredible Man.

My Brief Love Affair

For the first time in my life I had money of my own to spend. Up until my teaching year in Spangle, I never had an extra penny. Scrimping and saving had been a way of life for my family and me. I had started my savings account at the Cheney Bank while still in high school. A little of every paycheck always went into the bank. Suddenly I had extra money to spend. It was intoxicating. At first I was hesitant to splurge. However, it wasn't long before I found a way to spend it.

On Saturdays, I could ride the Greyhound bus from Spangle to Spokane for fifteen cents. Then an indulgent lunch at Newberry's Dime Store counter cost me one dollar. A stroll past the shops downtown was free, but soon I found myself staring in the shop windows at something that made my mouth water. I had fallen in love. I found myself involved in a sudden, serious, and insatiable affair with pretty shoes.

My earliest memories of shoes, when I was 4 or 5 years old and recovering from polio, were not happy ones. I was left with poor balance, and I had to wear ugly high-topped orthopedic shoes with a leg brace. They were supposed to improve my balance and correct my gait. I hated those shoes with a passion. I thought they looked like boy's shoes. I stared with green-eyed envy when I saw other little girls prancing by in their cute slippers or patent leather Mary Janes.

When I got to college, I managed to find a pair of sensible walking shoes that I could afford. They were size two and I bought them at a shoe shop in Spokane for ninety-five cents. My girlfriends at college often called me

149

"Little Girlie Two-Shoes" and admired my tiny feet.

It was probably no surprise that when I got my first paycheck from the Spangle School District, I went to Spokane to buy a pair of shoes. Mother had sewn a nice new dress for me. It was a sage green rayon, with a pleated skirt. I found a soft brown leather belt to wear with it and was delighted to find a pair of brown leather pumps that matched the color of the belt. I suddenly felt that I was the height of fashion. Monday morning I wore the dress and the shoes to school. It gave me so much confidence to step into my classroom looking so stylish.

In November, when I went to spend the Thanksgiving holiday with Earl in Seattle, I bought the perfect navy pumps to wear with my navy blue dress. I also bought the most adorable pair of frivolous high-heeled red sandals. I knew that Earl would be coming home to Cheney for the Christmas holidays and New Years Eve. The sandals would be perfect for dancing. I imagined myself, dazzling and elegant in red high heels, whirling and spinning on the dance floor with Earl.

Earl and his friend, Dick Butler, came over to Cheney early in December to spend a weekend at home. He and Dick took turns driving the long miles over the mountains. Dick was the sole support of his widowed mother, and he and Earl came home whenever they could. We spent much of that weekend together at Earl's ranch just taking long walks and dreaming about the future when we could be together all the time. On Sunday, December 7th, it was time for Earl and Dick to return to Seattle. We said our goodbyes early in the morning, and the boys drove off.

Shortly after eleven o'clock the news of Pearl Harbor came over the radio. I knew I had to get back to Spangle as soon as I could. Neither my folks nor Earl's had telephones, but I had one in Spangle. I was sure that Earl would call me as soon as he got to Seattle. As the grim news continued over the radio, I was fearful of what conditions Earl might find. I needed to hear from him and make sure that he was alright.

The news from Hawaii was shocking. The naval base at Pearl Harbor had been attacked by Japanese bombers and submarines. The attack happened around eight o'clock in the morning Hawaii time. Four battleships were sunk and four others were badly damaged. The Japanese also destroyed or damaged eight other ships and hundreds of airplanes. Casualty figures kept getting higher and higher as the day dragged on. Thousands of sailors were killed or wounded in the attack. We all knew that we were in the war now. The next day, on December 8, President Roosevelt and Congress would officially declare war on Japan. He called December 7th "a date which will live in infamy."

All kinds of wild rumors were already circulating. None of us on the east side of the state knew what was really going on in Seattle. The news on the radio was full of speculation. Seattle seemed to be very vulnerable to attack. The naval shipyards were in Bremerton nearby and Seattle also had Boeing Airplane Company where B-17's were made. They were both strategic targets.

My brother Don drove me to Spangle that afternoon. On the way we stopped at the Hilton Ranch, and I promised to keep in touch. It was seven o'clock in the evening when I got the call from Earl. He told me how they had arrived to find Seattle in total darkness. Only one light could be seen from the bluff in West Seattle that overlooked the waterfront. Seattle was hidden under a complete blackout. Rumors had spread rapidly that the west coast might soon come under attack.

Pearl Harbor changed everything. There would be no dancing that New Years Eve. My fancy red sandals were pushed to the back of the closet. The draft act of 1940 was amended to require all men from 18 to 65 to register for the draft with those aged 18 to 45 being liable for immediate induction into the army. The service commitment for inductees was set to the duration of the war plus six months. Earl could be called up at any time. Our bright future grew dimmer as winter snows began to pile up around Spangle.

Instead of pretty dancing slippers, I invested in a sturdy pair of rubber galoshes that slipped over my brown shoes. When fur coats went on sale after the holidays, Madelyn insisted I should buy one. She thought that there were two things a young professional woman should invest in: a fur coat and a diamond ring. Madelyn already had two of each and spent time putting them in and out of storage.

The colder it got, the more I realized that I did need a warm winter coat. However, there would be no frivolous fur for me. I bought a black wool coat with a fur collar, not too showy, but perfect for me. It was the first real winter coat I'd had in years. I also bought a red wool dress that I found at the Palace Store. The entire outfit cost me all the money I had allotted for myself for several months.

I tried to convince myself that these were essential items for the wardrobe of a professional woman as Madelyn propounded. But with the war on, we would all soon be asked to make sacrifices for our country. My season of spending money on myself had been a short one, barely three months had passed between my first paycheck and the attack on Pearl Harbor. Soon anything made of leather would be rationed. It would be a long time before I would buy another pair of pretty shoes.

Ernestine in black wool coat with fur collar & Earl
Earl liked my coat and liked to show it off.

The Morning after Pearl Harbor

Going to school the morning after Pearl Harbor was difficult. I went to my classroom early, not knowing what to expect. There was no time for a staff meeting. We teachers were on our own. The buses arrived on time. Worried little faces walked into the classroom. Some parents brought their children to school, reluctant to let them out of their sight.

I knew this was a moment that we would all remember. I wanted to make it a morning that would remind my pupils of the goodness of America and its strength and help calm their fears. My students were 9 and 10 years old, frightened and reluctant to leave their mothers and fathers and their homes. Their school needed to be a safe haven for them that day. Class work would have to be postponed while we talked things over.

I met each child at the classroom door. My little charges, fifteen in number, were agitated and uneasy. Some were talking belligerently, others were quiet, obviously uncertain and afraid. Although we had been together only three short months, I had come to know them quite well. I knew they loved to sing. As soon as the bell rang and everyone was in their seats, I stepped to the piano.

"Children, we all know that our country has been attacked," I said. "We are all worried and sad about what happened in Hawaii. Hawaii is far away in the Pacific Ocean, but it is a part of America."

I rolled down the big map above the blackboard so we could look at Hawaii, the spot on the map where the tragedy had struck. We could see that it was far away across the ocean.

"America is strong and our country will keep us safe," I told the children. "Before we begin our class work this morning, we need to take some time to talk about what has happened. We can talk about how we feel and what we are thinking. But first, let's begin as we always do, with a song. What song would you like to sing this morning?"

Hands shot up quickly. Kenny stood up. Usually boisterous and loud, Kenny turned quietly to face the row of windows that looked to the northeast. From the windows we could see the wheat fields where the grain had been harvested. The field of stubble lay golden in the shining morning sun. In the distance, Mica Peak could be seen, rearing its tree-covered head in the distant blue sky.

Quietly, Kenny said, "Please, Teach, can we sing *'America the Beautiful'*?"

I couldn't have chosen a better song. A chorus of "yeahs" followed. The class stood and turned their little faces toward the morning sun. Loud and clear, their voices rang out. I have never forgotten that moment, the little children singing, strong and confident. Perhaps they too would keep this moment in their hearts.

My classroom door opened and Irma Mae, with her first and second graders from across the hall, came to join us. We spent the first hour of that day singing and talking. There were many questions. It was good to think of others at a time like this.

Someone noticed that none of the Japanese students had come to school that day. We talked about how hard it must have been for them and how they might have been afraid to come to school. There were thirty-one students that attended our school from their homes in the Japanese Gardens along the banks of Hangman Creek near Spokane. I never saw them again. We knew all of them, and our hearts were sad, wondering what might have become of them.

Many Japanese immigrants had come to Spokane as railroad workers in the early 1900s. When railroad work ended, many returned to Japan. Those who stayed became farmers on leased land and worked hard to build lives for themselves. The bombing of Pearl Harbor sent a wave of fear through the Japanese community in the Spokane area. They had already endured long decades of discrimination in order to raise their families and work their farms in America.

When President Roosevelt signed the order to evacuate Japanese Americans from coastal regions, the Japanese population of Spokane suddenly tripled. Spokane was far enough inland to fall outside the evacuation area. Many Japanese immigrants fled to Spokane for the duration of the war.

As the weeks went on, people of Japanese ancestry were barred from approaching certain sensitive installations such as airfields. Some Japanese workers were fired from their jobs. However, Spokane proved to be a haven for first and second generation Japanese Americans. Young men were recruited into military intelligence when the Army realized that Japanese-speaking Americans were a valuable asset as translators and interrogators.

Although the Japanese American students did not return to class at Spangle School that year, they remained in their homes throughout the war, while a hundred thousand others were relocated to internment camps.

With the resiliency of youth, our students were soon back to normal, doing their school work and playing their games. There were times when talk at home about the war would worry them, and we would have to talk about it before we began our lessons at school.

Eighty Cents an Hour

Pearl Harbor changed all the ideas we had for our future. No longer would we be able to continue our lives according to our own plan. All of that blew away that awful day. Not driven to panic like many young couples, Earl and I tried to be sensible as we continued to move carefully into the unknown future.

When spring came and we could see the farmers out in the fields seeding their new crops from the wide windows of our school, I received a letter from Earl, reminding me that he was coming over from Seattle in a couple of weeks. He casually mentioned that his wages had increased to eighty cents an hour. That magic number. Then he invited me to the spring formal at the college.

I had never had a formal dress of my own. I always fashioned something from old dresses that belonged to someone else. This time I wanted a dress of my own. On Saturday I went shopping. I chose a floor-length white taffeta dress that would show off my brown hair. It had an overskirt printed with red carnations that gave the dress an elegant look. I found my red high-heeled sandals in the back of the closet. They had never been worn.

On May 23, 1942, Earl drove from Seattle to Spangle. He strolled casually into my classroom just as school was closing for the day. Much to the delight of the children, he teased them as they gathered around him. Kenny, who lived just down the road from Earl's folks, spoke up.

"That's Teach's boyfriend," he declared, pointing at Earl. "He's the guy that lives down the road from my house. He is going to marry Teach!"

The whole class collapsed with laughter as they crowded around us. Earl and I couldn't keep from laughing too.

The next evening, when Earl came to pick me up wearing his new blue suit, I introduced him to the Grunewalds. As we drove off to the dance that evening, Earl turned off onto Depot Springs Road. I thought we were going to his house to see his folks. Instead he pulled up at the wooden pasture gate at the Rocky Pine Ranch off Depot Springs Road. There, with the sweet smell of wild roses blooming in the lane around us, he took the diamond ring from his pocket and asked me to marry him and be the mother of his children.

Of course I said yes. He slipped the ring on my finger and pinned a beautiful corsage of red roses and white carnations on my shoulder. Then we went happily off to the college dance, thrilled at the prospect of our life together. The next day we told our parents and set the date for our wedding for September 13th, the date of his parents' anniversary.

Earl & Ernestine May 24, 1942
Earl was acting pretty smug once he got the ring on my finger. Note, he has a new car.

Earl drove back to Seattle, and I went back to my classroom. In those days, married women could not teach in Washington State schools. On Monday, I turned in my resignation, canceling next year's contract that I had already signed. My year as a teacher would soon be over. Tearfully, I invited my little students to our September wedding.

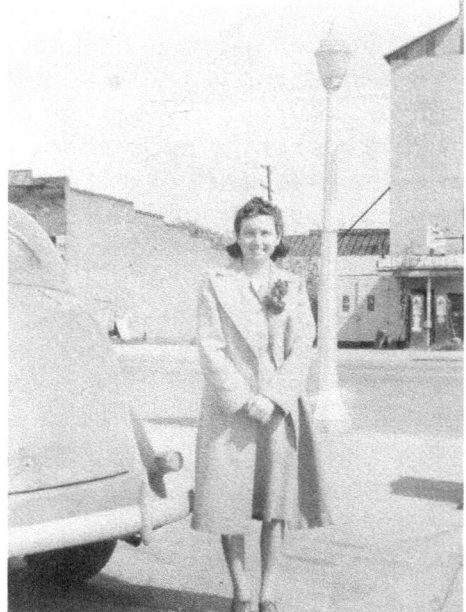

Earl & Ernestine May 25, 1942
The next morning after the Spring Formal in Cheney, seeing Earl off for Seattle
The ring was on my finger. We were both very happy.

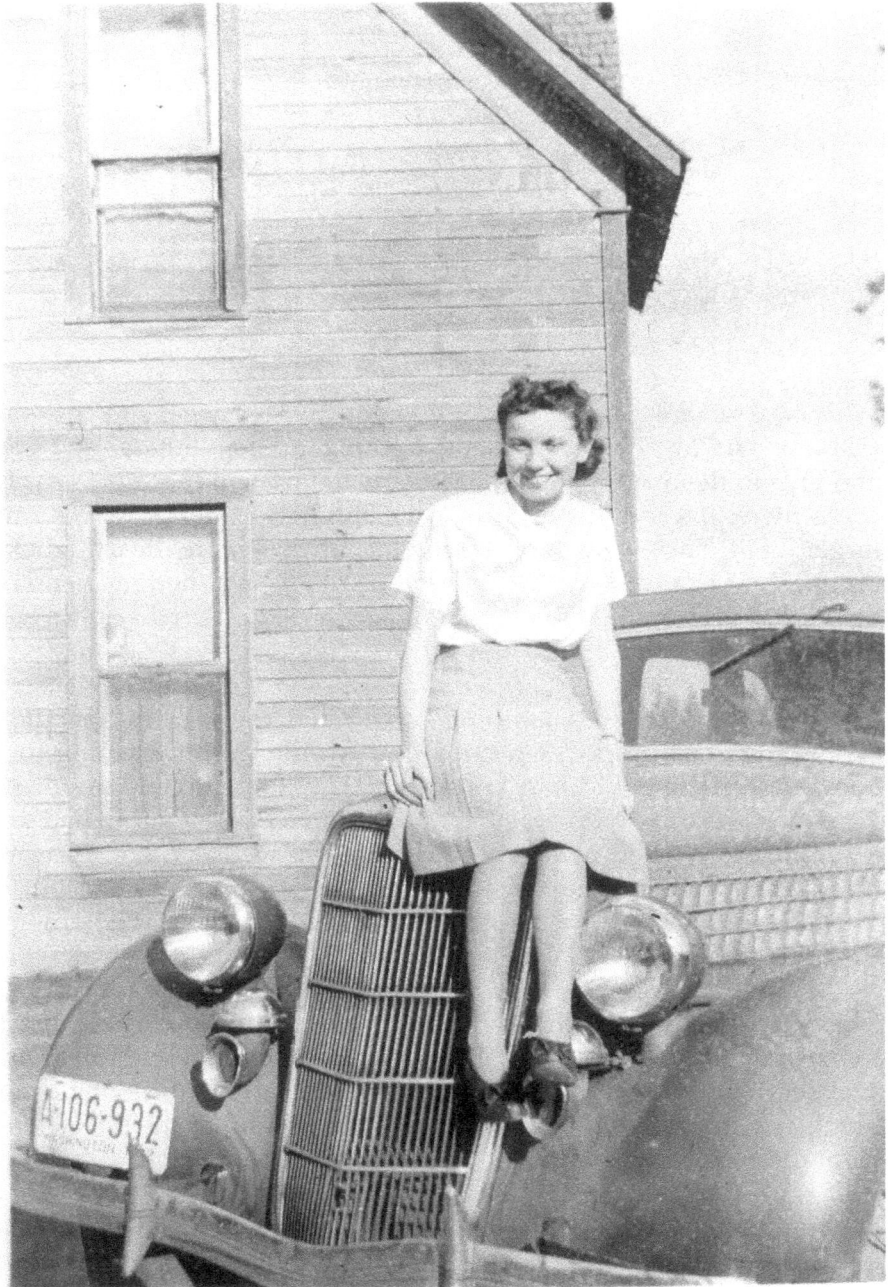

Ernestine at Rocky Pine Ranch after accepting Earl's proposal

Father Comes to Fetch Me

When the school year was over I spent my last weekend in Spangle cleaning out my desk at school, packing up my things, and saying goodbye to the many people I had come to know in the short year I had spent there. I knew I would miss the children I taught. I would never forget them. They were a part of my life, always in my heart. I took one last look at Mica Peak from the row of windows, brushed my hands over my empty desk and left the room quickly, afraid to turn back, tears were too close.

I had always planned a teaching career, and my year in Spangle was everything I had hoped. I wished that I could go on teaching for just a few more years. Yet I had known Earl, my Incredible Man, for seven years. We had grown up together and our love for each other had grown up with us. We had always known that we were looking forward to marriage, but the war gave us very little chance to have things our way. We both understood the dangers Earl faced. Our love was strong and true. The time was now.

I was surprised when Father came alone to bring me home. He carried my things out to the trunk of his car. With handshakes and hugs all around, I said goodbye to Lizzie and John Gruenwald. I left them waving from the porch as we coasted down the street to the bottom of the hill where the giant grain elevator stood. My life in Spangle was over.

Looking back toward the town, I knew that I would never forget it. I loved the children, the town's people, and even the very land itself. I

160

loved the Palouse country with its endless rolling hills where the tiny town of Spangle was tucked in at the edge of the wide prairie. I was a farm girl, born and bred, and the land lived within me. It was hard to turn my back on those waving fields of grain, green and promising.

Spangle Washington
Photo by Alison Hilton, 2011

It was a warm June day, the windows were rolled down, and we enjoyed the drive toward home. When we crossed the railroad tracks and came into Cheney, Father pulled up at the big grange supply store. I expected him to gas up the car. But instead he coasted around the side of the building, parked in the shade and shut off the motor.

Suspecting that father had stopped to get some chicken feed or supplies of some sort, I sat silently in the car. But instead he turned to me and began to talk. First he asked if I felt comfortable about turning back my teaching contract. We discussed the fact that only single women could teach. Having been a school board member, Father knew perfectly well what the rules were.

I didn't quite understand what he was trying to tell me. So I explained to him that my promise to those who provided my scholarship required only that I teach one year in a Washington state school. I had fulfilled the requirement successfully. We sat quiet for a moment. Then Father told me what was on his mind.

"I'm concerned about you giving up your job now when the situation with the war is so grave. Earl will probably be drafted soon. Now that America is in it, many more men are going to be needed. War is a serious business. There's a chance that Earl won't make it back, and you could be left alone with a child to raise."

"Of course I've thought about that," I explained to Father. "Earl and I both have. We have discussed it over and over again, many times. Even before I went teaching. We knew the consequences all along. On my visit to Seattle for Thanksgiving, we selected our rings. Pearl Harbor hasn't changed our plans to marry. We have already made our decision to have some time together. Earl's chance of another deferment are slim. We're willing to face what may come."

We sat silently in the car. Finally Father spoke again. "All right. I am glad to know that you have thought all this over. I didn't set out to talk you out of marrying Earl. He's a fine young man. I just wanted to be sure that you understood what might happen."

He started the car and drove on. I felt rather sorry that I hadn't talked this over with Father earlier. I had been out on my own for so long. I was 22 years old and accustomed to making my own decisions. I had always turned to Father when I needed advice. I felt a little guilty for not including him in my decision, but this was a matter that was entirely mine to decide.

"I'm sorry to worry you," I told him as we parked under the elm tree at Hilltop Place.

I hugged him fiercely. Father seemed satisfied. It was just like him to worry about me. Now I understood why he had chosen to come alone to bring me home from Spangle. Father would always have my welfare at heart. And I would always be his grateful daughter.

Wheat hills near Spangle, Mica Peak in the background
Photo by Alison Hilton, 2011

My Friend Clare

When Clare and I were about to finish college, she learned she was lacking two credits to graduate. Although she was allowed to graduate with our class in June of 1941, she had to go back summer quarter to get her teaching certificate. She completed her work in early August and secured a teaching position in Toppenish, Washington. She would be teaching freshman English and French, just as she had always dreamed.

Her favorite Aunt Elsa lived only 60 miles from Toppenish in Pasco near the small farming town of Richland. Before the onset of World War II, the population of Richland hovered at about 300. As WWII started heating up, the US Army purchased 640 square miles of land on the Columbia River, displacing some of the town's residents. Richland began to grow rapidly as scientists, technicians, and engineers poured into the town with their families. They came to work at the Hanford Engineer Works. Hanford was part of the top-secret Manhattan Project.

Clare's aunt kept a boarding house in Pasco and had several young scientists living with her. Clare often visited her aunt on the weekends. During one of those visits she met a young scientist who was working on the secret project at Hanford.

Clare and I wrote often and she was the first person I told that I was giving up my teaching job to marry Earl. When the school year ended, Clare returned to Cheney and I learned that she was engaged to her young scientist. Her teaching contract was also terminated and she came home to plan her summer wedding. We spent our summer days shopping and dreaming of our upcoming weddings.

Late in June, Clare and I went to Spokane to shop for wedding gowns. She and her father drove into Cheney that morning where I met them. Her father had business appointments in Spokane so he continued on his way while Clare and I drove to Spokane in my father's car. Clare's father said he would meet us back in Cheney at 4:00 pm.

When we got back to Cheney that afternoon, we waited but her father did not return. Clare called home but no one answered. We waited until it was dark which was quite late on the June evening. We asked all over downtown, but no one had seen him. We inquired at the bus station, thinking maybe he might have had car trouble and come back on the bus. I offered to take Clare home, but she was quite upset and determined to wait. We parked on Main Street and waited. Another hour went by. Clare called home, but again there was no answer.

We didn't know what to do. Finally, Mr. Jerue, a local businessman, suggested we go see Clare's mother's best friend, Mrs. Bernard, who lived a few blocks away on Third Street. We drove up to the Bernard home hoping to find her father there. Instead, we found her mother. She told Clare that her father was dead. He had collapsed and died on the street in Spokane that morning.

I offered to drive Clare and her mother home. On the way her mother told us that she and Mr. Findley had planned to divorce. Clare had not been aware of any problems between them and this news was an additional shock. Clare begged me to stay with her that night. She was very upset and couldn't understand what had happened to her parents' relationship or why her father had died so suddenly.

Before we went upstairs to her room, Clare called her brother, Herbert. He was in the Air Force stationed in Great Falls, Montana. He promised to come home at once. Grief-stricken and in shock, Clare barricaded us in her room. With me beside her, we spent a restless night. Clare went over and over what could have happened between her parents in the time that she had been away. She loved her father dearly and they were very close. She had a distant and strained relationship with her mother but had always assumed that her parents were happy together.

I kept my own council. Although I had always found her parents pleasant, they were much different from mine. They were always very formal and polite with each other but I sensed that they did not share the easy affection and love the way my parents did.

The next morning when her brother arrived, their mother got in the car and left the ranch, saying she was going to stay with her sister in Spokane. She left the funeral arrangements entirely up to Clare and her brother. I stayed to help. Her father was well known in Cheney and she and her brother planned a fine graveside service. She called her fiancé in Richland and he came immediately to be with her.

The day after her father's burial, with her brother Herbert and me as attendants, Clare and Walt Gerin were married at the Spokane County Courthouse. It was not the gorgeous wedding that Clare had dreamed of surrounded by friends and family. She was sad and exhausted but also looking forward to her new life. There was little time for grieving. We both knew that our young men could be called away from us at any time and we had to live in the moment as much as possible.

A week later, Clare and her mother agreed on a settlement of things in the house. The newlyweds borrowed the farm truck, loaded the things they chose to take, and went to live in Longview, Washington where Walt took a position as a forest timber cruiser for Pope and Talbot Lumber Company.

We wrote to each other faithfully, sharing our troubles and triumphs both large and small. Our friendship had been forged through all the years of growing up in difficult times. The sadness of her father's sudden death stayed with me as I finished the planning and preparation for my own wedding that was just a few weeks away.

Two Weddings

It was a hot August morning in 1942. The last of the invitations were in the mail, and I was busy with preparations for our wedding, just ten days away. I was suddenly roused from my work by the roar of Earl's car, barreling up the road to the house. Before I could reach the door, Earl rushed in.

Taking me in his arms, he said, "Please come with me. I want us to go to Seattle and get married."

In his hand he was clutching a manila envelope. I recognized it at once. It was a draft notice from Uncle Sam.

"I don't want to go into the army without assurance that you will be cared for. I want us to be married so right from the start you will get benefits from the army."

We had talked about this often. Earl had friends who got married after they went into the service. Often it took months before their wives received their allotment from the government. It was especially difficult if there were no children involved. If you were married when you went into the army, the wives had no problem receiving their benefits.

Earl was especially concerned about this now that I had terminated my teaching contract. He felt responsible for taking me away from teaching. He had watched me struggle through college. He felt that he was now completely responsible for my welfare. He wanted to make sure that I would be treated properly. So, from what he had heard from his friends, he wasn't taking any chances.

Doran's Machine Shop was a long-time navy supply company. They made vital parts for battleships. They were confident that they could secure a deferment for Earl, since their work was critical to the war effort. But the war was ramping up and the army was recruiting as fast as possible. Earl knew that Uncle Sam was breathing down his neck. Doran Company was confident that they could keep him out of the war. But Earl wasn't so sure.

"I only have a few days off. Please come with me," he said.

We had only to look into each other's eyes. Of course I would marry him, anytime, anywhere. I knew that. He knew that. I went upstairs to my room, took one last, longing look at the beautiful white satin wedding gown hanging in my closet, grabbed my going-away suit and a nightgown, stuffed them into a bag and rushed back down stairs.

After only a few minutes spent explaining to my mother, we climbed into the Ford and sped off. Looking back I saw Mother standing at the gate. Her hand was shading her eyes, a look of complete bewilderment drawn on her face. She waved goodbye as we drove away.

We were in a such a rush, but Earl had it all figured out. There was a three day waiting period to marry after you got your license. We already had gotten our license in Spokane. We could use it to get married in Seattle, but we would have to get another license for our Cheney wedding. Since it was Friday, we would have to get to the King County Courthouse in Seattle before they closed.

We quickly decided on a wedding party to accompany us. We stopped at Rocky Pine Ranch where Earl's mother and his cousin Renee joined us. We laughed at the idea of his mother coming along on our honeymoon. It was a swift drive over the mountains to Seattle. We arrived at the courthouse just in time to get another marriage license before it closed for the weekend. Earl had called ahead to his cousins in West Seattle, where we stopped just long enough to hurry into our wedding attire.

Wedding party
Earl's mother Lura Hilton, Ernestine, Earl's cousin Renee Franks

Seaview Methodist Church West Seattle

We were married that evening, September 2, 1942, in the Minister's study in the West Seattle Seaview Methodist Church where Earl had gone to Sunday school as a child. Earl's cousins, Renee and Bob, were our attendants. As we stood together, Earl looked so handsome in his navy blue suit. He pinned a beautiful orchid on the shoulder of my going away outfit. Everyone began to laugh as the orchid bounced up and down with each beat of my heart. The minister frowned and reminded us that this was a solemn occasion.

We held hands and looked into each other's eyes as we spoke the sacred words of our marriage. Sincere were the vows, solemnly spoken. We had known each other for a long time. We were ready for marriage.

Following the brief service, we returned to cousin Bob's home for a jolly round of cake and drinks. After our little supper we went down to spend our weekend honeymoon in the old Moore Hotel. It was lucky that Earl had called earlier that morning for a reservation. As we stepped into the lobby of the hotel, we encountered what appeared to be the entire Pacific Fleet.

There were sailors everywhere. They were asleep on the couches and sprawled on the floor, heads resting on seabags. We had to step over bodies everywhere. Our new status must have been pretty obvious, because we got lots of loud whistles and shouts as we maneuvered our way across the lobby.

We returned to Cheney Sunday evening with mother-in-law in tow. We never said anything to my brothers and sister about our hasty marriage, although our parents knew of the Seattle wedding. As it turned out, Earl was not called up immediately as we had feared. So we decided to go ahead with our original wedding plans. The evening before our formal wedding, we held a rehearsal dinner at my parents' home with many of our old friends.

It was wartime and food was rationed. Mother managed to make her wonderful spaghetti and her warm homemade bread. The usually quiet Earl got a rousing cheer when he arrived dressed in jeans, a cowboy hat and spurs, singing a popular song of the day.

"I got spurs that jingle, jangle, jingle
And they say, 'Oh ain't you glad your single',
And that song ain't so very far from wrong."

When he began to sing another favorite western song of his *"Don't Fence Me In,"* everybody chimed in singing and laughing at Earl's high jinks.

The next evening, September 13th, we were solemnly married again in the small Christian church on the college campus. None of the guests knew that it was our second wedding. It was a beautiful wedding that ended with lots of laughs when Earl accidentally knocked off my veil when he kissed me. I was well and truly married.

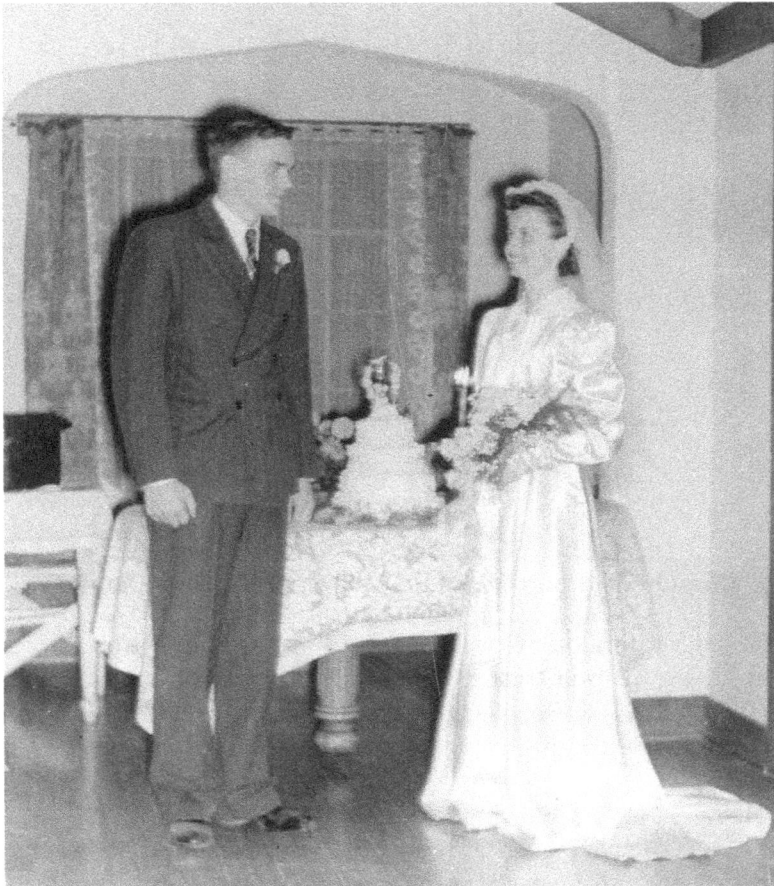

Earl & Ernestine wedding day September 13, 1942

Later, in the minister's study, Earl held my hand tightly and said nothing when our minister signed our marriage certificate.

Looking up at us, the minister said casually, "Hmm – Seattle. I thought I saw your notice in the Spokane paper?"

Nothing more was said. Our reception at my home was wonderful. Mrs. Lauff baked the wedding cake in her famous Cheney bakery. Covered with delicate cream-colored roses to match my bouquet, it was delicious.

Cheney Wedding Christian Church on College Campus

Late that night after our wedding reception, attended by many friends and family, we heaped the car with wedding presents and sped off for Seattle. It was time for Earl to get back to work. At the top of the hill that led down the winding highway to cross the Columbia River at Vantage, the car ran out of gas.

Earl pulled to the side of the road. A big harvest moon beamed over us in the midnight sky. There beside the road, by the light of the full moon shining down on the river below, we hugged and kissed and dined on cold chicken, wedding cake and punch from the box that mother thrust into our hands as we rushed out of the house. We were married. Not once but twice. We giggled at the thought that it might take two divorces to get us out of this.

Then Earl poured gas into our stalled car from a can he had thoughtfully put in the trunk, and we proceeded on to an Ellensburg hotel. The next morning we drove on to Seattle and Earl went back to work at Doran's, and I checked into the Moore Hotel.

Cheney Wedding Party taken in McMillan home on Granite Lake Road
Doris Jean Spence, Lucille Billisbach, Sister Edith, Ernestine, Earl, Best man Dick Butler, Brothers Don, and Ted

Housing was extremely tight during the war years, and we had no place to go. Hotel stays were limited to five nights. So I spent the next four days frantically searching for an apartment. Every morning I poured over the ads in the papers and spent the day on the trolley, riding to and fro in the unfamiliar city.

The fifth and final day at the Moore Hotel, I found a decent place for us. It was a studio apartment on Fourth Street. A glimpse of the Seattle harbor was visible from the kitchen window, and a peak of the Olympic Mountains across Puget Sound could be seen from the living room. The sounds of mournful foghorns and the whistles of the ferryboats leaving the docks became our background music as we set up housekeeping. It was there that we spent the first happy year of our marriage.

In the meantime, the company Earl worked for had gotten a temporary reprieve for him, so he continued to work at Doran's making ship parts for the U.S. Navy. Earl was skillful in mathematics and quickly learned how to manage and set the machinery used there.

Bored with being home alone, I soon secured a job at Allied Building Credits, the real estate division of the Weyerhaeuser Corporation. I began as a cashier at the front desk, but when it became known that my Spangle school superintendent was a college classmate of my new boss, I moved into the back room as secretary to the president of the company. My salary was three times what I made as a teacher, $300 a month. It was a fortune.

As newlyweds we embraced life in the city. We both had good jobs and lofty ambitions. The war lurked just out of sight as we enjoyed the entertainment and excitement of Seattle. We spent our evenings downtown soaking up the nightlife. It was a whirlwind of frantic fun. We attended the theater, musical events, the movies and dined in the finest restaurants.

A Delayed Honeymoon

It was September again, and the first blissful year of our marriage had passed. We were deeply in love. The war was still breathing down our necks. Earl hadn't had a day off work since our wedding. We had no time for a proper honeymoon. Gas rationing made any idea of a trip seem impossible.

Earl knew that I'd never been to the ocean. I had read about it and heard about it and longed to see it. He knew how disappointed I was when Father refused to let me go down the coast to see the San Francisco World's Fair with Clare. Earl always promised that someday he would take me to the ocean. My desire to see the ocean began when I was a child. Relatives had come to our house bringing a seashell from their vacation on Cape Cod.

"Hold it up to your ear and listen to the ocean roar," Cousin Millie said as she put the shell into my hand.

"Touch the glass with your tongue and taste the salt of the sea," said Cindy, as she gave me a handful of the sea-tossed glass she found on the beach. From then on I was fascinated with the ocean. From our apartment I watched the ships go in and out from the Seattle waterfront, wondering what it would be like to sail out onto the Pacific Ocean.

One Friday morning Earl gave me an extra hug when he kissed me goodbye, then he raced down the stairs on his way to work. He stopped on the steps and called back.

"Honey, pack a suitcase with our swimsuits and warm jackets. Be ready when I come home this afternoon. We are going on a honeymoon."

A honeymoon this afternoon? Earl liked to surprise me, coming up with wild ideas of ways to spend our free time together. I knew he was completely serious about going on a honeymoon. I was ready and waiting when he turned the key in the lock and walked in the door. It had been a year since our wedding. Earl had plotted this surprise and I knew it would be fun.

Ernestine & Earl in front of their first apartment on 4th Ave in Seattle
Photo taken on their 50th wedding anniversary, September, 1992

The water of Puget Sound slapped against the ferry as we drove our car down onto the car deck. A loud blast of the boat's whistle shattered the air as we raced up the stairs onto the passenger deck. We stood at the rail with our arms around each other, the salty spray flying into our faces as the boat pulled away from the dock. A haze hung over the top of Mount Rainier as we gazed back at Seattle dwindling away behind the boat.

We ate fish and chips with our fingers and fed the leftovers to the seagulls that followed the ferry as it ploughed up the inland waters of Puget Sound. The boat stopped in Port Angeles on the north side of the Olympic Peninsula, and we drove off the ferry.

The late sun shone through the tall firs as we drove down Highway 101 along beautiful Lake Crescent and out to the ocean at Ruby Beach. Suddenly, there it was, my first glimpse of the ocean and the seashore. When we parked the car I heard the pounding surf. Earl held me tightly as we watched the waves come crashing to the shore. I was overwhelmed by the smell of the salty sea air, the pounding of the surf, and the majesty of it all.

Then Earl took my hand and we ran along the sandy shore, watching the waves dash in and out, rippling across the warm sand. When we tired of playing tag with the surf, we sank down in the shade of a log. As the sun faded into the ocean we watched and listened. The ocean rolled on. The tide came in. A brisk wind blew, lifting the waves high into the air and crashing them upon the shore.

"Roll on, oh mighty ocean roll on!" I hummed softly to myself, remembering an old song from many years ago. The ocean was all that I had imagined. We spent the weekend there in a little cabin on a sandy spit. It was a wonderful honeymoon, despite the fact that it was a year late. My dream of seeing the ocean had come true.

On the way back on the ferry, we began to talk about our wonderful trip. We wished we had someone with us to share our delight. It was not the companionship of friends or relations that we were missing. After all, which of our friends would we really want to bring along? We looked at each other and we knew. We wanted a baby. One month later I was pregnant with our first child.

We were busy making plans for our family when we got the bad news. The Draft Board had rejected Doran's request for a continued deferment for Earl. It came as a rude awakening. Earl was now classified 1-A. He was eligible to be called up for service. It was only a few days later when Earl received a letter to report to Fort Lewis, Washington. He was given a thirty day furlough before reporting for duty.

That left us just four short weeks to prepare ourselves for what lay ahead. The fact that we had always known this might happen didn't make it any easier. We vowed not to spend any of our precious time together crying and tried to make every moment special. Earl got busy arranging our affairs, and I resigned from my job as private secretary to the president of Weyerhaeuser.

Earl's fellow workers at Doran Company gave him a big sendoff party, and at the end of the furlough, we loaded as many of our belongings as we could into our Ford and sped across the mountains to Cheney. When the time came for Earl to report for duty, my brother Don insisted that he accompany Earl back to Seattle on the train to see him off to Fort Lewis where he reported for duty with about forty other young men from Washington State.

I went with them to the train station in Cheney where we stood in the cold and foggy December morning, holding each other tight, listening for the train whistle as it came down the track. We didn't cry when we kissed goodbye and Earl climbed aboard. I stood on the platform alone in the cold, watching the train until it was out of sight.

From Fort Lewis Earl was assigned to Company B, 13th Battalion, 20th Armored Division in the Third Army under General George Patton. He left Fort Lewis, heading for Fort Knox, Kentucky, on December 20, 1943, just five days before Christmas.

Baby Just in Time

Earl and I had discussed where I should stay while he was in the army. We both agreed it would be best for me to go home to my parents. His parents lived only ten miles away. I was glad to be back with our families. I was pleased that Dr. West, our old family doctor, would be caring for me and the baby that was due in July. It was an upsetting time for us both, so before Earl left to report to Fort Lewis, we went for a visit with the doctor.

When Dr. West and I came out of the examination room, he went straight to Earl and shook his hand. "It is my opinion that you can expect to have a healthy baby. Ernestine is in good health and everything looks fine. Have you ever seen a newborn baby?"

"Not people babies," Earl replied. "I've seen lots of baby calves being born. I grew up on a farm and helped with the birthing."

"Helped with the birthing?" the old Doc asked, squinting up at Earl.

"Yes sir," Earl replied with a grin.

"Well son," the old Doctor said, "tell you what. You being off to the service, this is what I'll do. When Ernestine goes into labor, I will send a telegram to your commanding officer asking for your support. We will see if we can get you home to see that new baby. It's my guess that it's going to be a boy."

Thrilled at the prospect of being together for the birth of our baby, Earl went off to camp, vowing to always have enough money in his pocket to take the train as soon as the telegram arrived.

Earl began his service in the army at Fort Knox, Kentucky where, due to his studies in mathematics, he was assigned to teach in the Gunnery School. This kept him out of the rigorous training that took place in his tank battalion. In June, shortly before the baby came, Earl was transferred to Camp Campbell, Kentucky. His battalion of the 20th Tank Division was taking special training, preparing them to ship out to Europe to join the Battle of the Bulge.

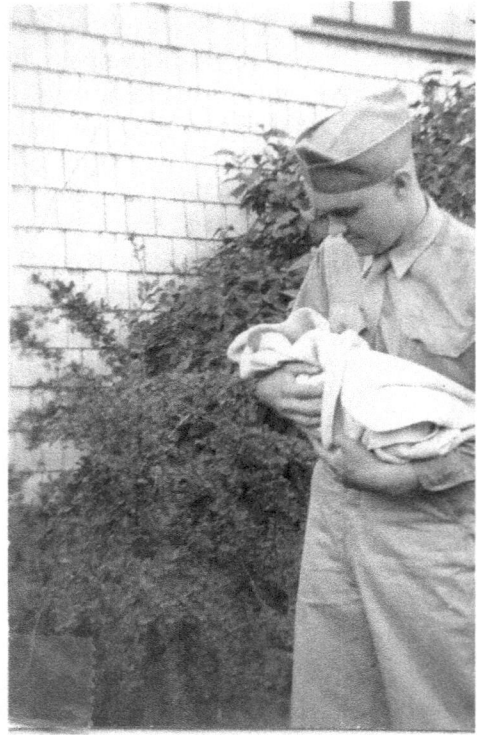

Ernestine and Earl with baby Earl Junior, July 1944

I went into labor in my parents' home on the last day of June, 1944. Dr. West was an old-fashioned country doctor, and he came out to the farm himself to take me to the hospital in Spokane. He immediately sent a telegram to Earl's commanding officer asking that Earl come to my bedside. I spent the long hours of my labor waiting and walking the hospital corridors with my mother and sister taking turns with me.

When Earl received the telegram he immediately set out by train for Spokane. It was a long trip, and the baby was three days old by the time Earl arrived. My nurse helped me into my pink bed jacket and bundled baby Earl Junior into his blue blanket. Then she pulled the curtains shut around my bed to give us some privacy. The whole ward shouted and clapped when Earl, in his army uniform, came into the room.

I was released to go home from the hospital when the baby was a week old so Earl could get acquainted with his namesake. It was a wonderful time to be together. We would stay with my folks a few days, then go to spend time with Earl's parents. Everyone helped care for the baby. We felt like a family again.

Grandma McMillan, Ernestine, Earl Junior and Grandma Hilton

Back at camp, Earl wrote me that while he was on furlough his unit had shipped overseas to fight in the Battle of the Bulge. He felt sure that the birth of the baby had saved his life. Earl was reassigned to a new unit and began training with a group preparing to go overseas.

In the fall he was able to get a furlough and spend fifteen days with us. The baby was sitting up and clapping his little hands. He was living up to his nickname, Sunny. He was a happy little boy with a sunny personality. We took him with us to Seattle where we visited with friends and relatives, and Earl showed off his fine son to his friends at Doran's. Having to leave us to go back to Camp Campbell was really hard for Earl. We clung to each other, reluctant to say goodbye. That time we

Earl, Ernestine and Sunny

both cried. Back at camp, Earl wrote home daily, begging me to come to him. He realized that his outfit was gearing up to move out. He was not emotionally ready to fight a war. He was having a very bad time.

Ernestine, Sunny and Earl
Taken in Seattle when Earl was on furlough, Fall 1944

Hoptown

In September, 1944, I received the following letter from Earl.

Saturday Morning September 9, 4:30 AM

Dear Erny,

Don't get too mad because of this letter. I guess I am about half lit or should be. There is something that I would like to know and that is, is it possible for you to come to Campbell? I would like to get an answer on the question. I want you to come awful bad. I don't know why it should be any worse now than it has been. But I guess I have been waiting until the kid was born and old enough to travel before I let the desire of having you to come and live near camp.

I realize it may be very foolish to expect you able in a position (mostly) to come down. But the main thing that I really want to know is it at all possible to come down I want to know if I can plan on it.

I want to know the facts. It is not that I hold it against you if you don't see your way possible to come. But I get tired of planning that sometime you will be able to come. I would rather know if it is possible for you to come, or not. I think it would be easier to face. I am sorry I can't help you much, my hands are tied. I can't even tell you where or how long we will be anywhere, so we could make plans.

All I know is we are going back to Campbell and will be there the 18th of Sept. So if you are able to come to a definite or more definite answer, I think it will

184

be better for both of us. We are leaving tonight, so the next address is Camp Campbell. Hope I didn't frighten or make you mad.   Love Earl

The United States Army ★ ★ ★

*Sat morning
Sept
9:30 AM*

Dear Emy,

Don't get too mad because of this letter. I guess I am about half lit or should be.

There is something that I would like to know and that is is it possible for you to come to Campbell. I would like to get an answer on the question. I want you to come awful bad. I don't know why it should be any worst now than it has been. But I guess I have been waiting until the kid was born and old enough to travel before I let the desire of having you to come and live near camp. I realize it maybe very foolish to expect you able in a position (mostly) to come down. But the main thing that I really want to know is it at all possible to come down. I just want to know if I can plan on it.

I would like it know the facts.
It is not that I hold it against you
if you don't see your way possible
to come. But I get tried of planning
that sometime you will be able
to come. I would rather know
if it was possible for you to come
or not. I think it would be easier
to face. I am sorry I can't help
you much, but my hand are tied
I can't even tell you where or
how long we will be anywhere
so you could make plans.

All I know is we are going back
to Campbell and will be there the
18th of Sept for a big 2nd Army
inspection. Just another inspection to
give some of the big boys something to
use their brass.

So if you are able to come
to a definite are more difinite answer
I think it will be better for
the both of us.

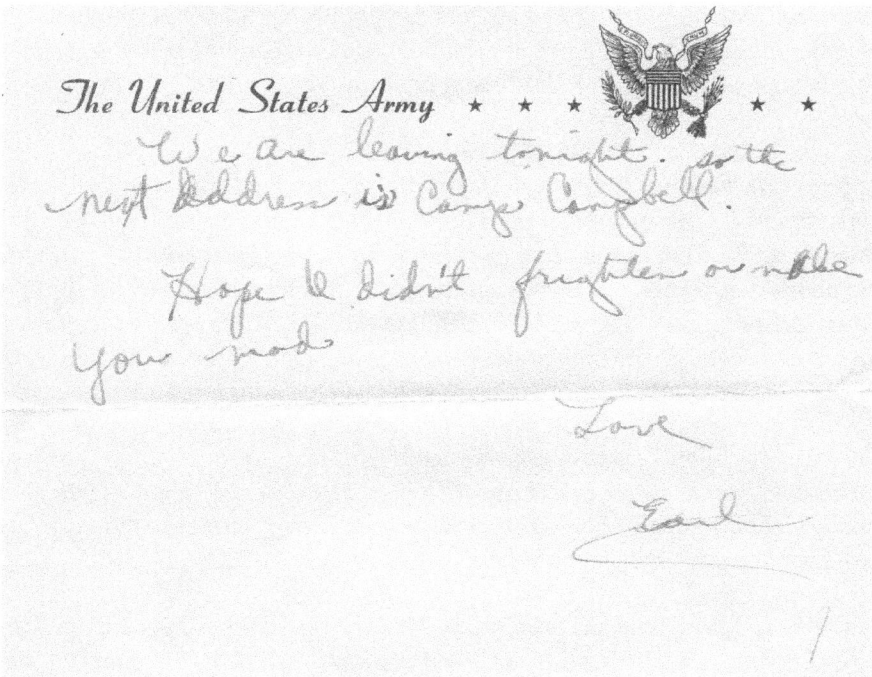

The United States Army ★ ★ ★

We are leaving tonight. so the next address is Camp Campbell.

Hope I didn't frighten or rattle you mad

Love

Earl

When I received Earl's letter, I knew that we needed to be together. I longed to be with him too, and I made up my mind to join him in Kentucky.

Dearest Earl,

Yes my darling, I will come. Just as soon as you say I can I'll send you $50 today to find us a place to live. I will come as soon as you say. I'd like to have a place to live when I get there, but if you can't find anything, get us a hotel room. Maybe then I could get something after I get there. I'm going to ask the Dr. today about taking the baby. I'm sure it will be all right. If not, I will wean him & leave him here & come down by myself for awhile anyway. I hope I don't have to leave the kid, & I don't think I will.

There isn't any reason why I shouldn't come, I don't see, honey. Money is the main angle, & we can manage that some way. I would live on bread & milk to be with you. I want to come as bad as you want me to darling. It's just the same with me as it is with you.

Congratulations Private First Class Hilton. Kiss you & kiss you. Aren't you something. Darling darling I'm so glad for you & awful proud of you too, my sweet ole hubby. How I'd like to see that stripe. And I intend to just as soon as I can. I'm so glad you got it, because you have deserved it for a long time, oh Earl Earl.

The folks will buy my ticket back there, round trip. Dad just said so. I will go compartment if I can get one, if not I'll go Pullman. Then we will have our $125. to live on at the first - or as long as it lasts, minus $50 I'm sending you today. How about your other account? Can we use that too? I know your folks would help us out too if we'd ask them, because they would like to see us together. I'm sure we can manage the money okay, at least we won't starve. We may not be able to go out very much, but maybe we will be glad enough to be together not to have to go out too much. Soon as the baby's money comes thru we will be okay. After Oct. 2nd you can cash war bonds at any bank & don't take 3 mo. so if anything bad came up we could resort to that. Heck, honey, some people go live together & don't have a cent but their allowance & no relatives to fall back on, so I don't see how very much could happen to us.

The worst is getting the kid back there. He'll be fine after we get there I know. And I think he won't even know he's making a trip. I'll be a little nervous about traveling with him, but when I get on to it, it will be swell.

Could it be at all possible for you to meet us in Chicago if we can come on a week-end? If not we can make it okay. I guess I can hardly wait to see you. We have to go from there down by day coach. How long does it take from Chicago? What town would we go to, Nashville? I wish we could live in Hoptown or Clarksville cause they are smaller, but I don't really care, I will live anywhere you can get us a place.

When should we come? You let me know when to come & we will. I'll ask Dr. about the baby this afternoon. & tell you what he says. Would be best if we know that you were going to be there at least a month, but I will come down when you say, regardless. By Oct. 1, he will be eating vegetables & maybe my milk would be all the extra he needs, & that would be swell because I wouldn't have to worry about his food. My milk is pretty strong.

PS: In town - P. Office. Baby on my knee. Dr. says perfectly OK to travel. Will make reservations for bedroom soon as you say when. Write more tonight. Jr. weighs 13 lbs 7 oz.

Love you Erny

Tues.
Sept. 12.

Dearest Earl,

Yes my darling, I will come.
Just as soon as you say I can.
I'll send you $50. today to find us
a place to live. I will come as soon
as you say. I'de like to have a place
to live when I get there, but if you can't
find anything, get us a hotel room.
Maybe then I could get something
after I got there. I'm going to ask
the Dr. today about taking the baby.
I'm sure it will be all right. If
not, I will wean him & leave him
here & come down by myself for awhile
anyway. I hope I don't have to leave the
kid, & I don't think I will.

There isn't any reason why I shouldn't
come, I don't see, honey. Money is the
main angle, & we can manage that
some way. I would live on bread &
milk to be with you. I want to

come as bad as you want me to, darling.
Its just the same with me as it is with
you.

Congratulations Private First Class Hilton.
Kiss you & kiss you. Aren't you something.
Darling darling I'm so glad for you & awful
proud of you too. my sweet ole hubby.
How I'de like to see that stripe. And I
intend to just as soon as I can. I'm
so glad you got it, because you have
deserved it for a long time. oh Earl Earl

The folks will buy my ticket back
there, round trip. Dad just said so.
I will go compartment if I can get one,
if not I'll go Pullman. Then we will
have our $125. to live on ~~this~~ at first — or
as long as it lasts (minus $50 I'm sending
you today. How about your other account?
Can we use that too? I know your
folks would help us out too if we'de
ask them, because they would like to
see us together. I'm sure we can

I manage the money okay, at least we won't starve. We may not be able to go out very much, but maybe we will be glad enough to be together not to have to go out too much. Soon as the baby's money comes then we will be okay. After Oct. 2. you can cash war bonds at any bank & don't take 3 mo., so if anything bad came up we could resort to that. Heck, honey, some people go live together & don't have a cent but their allowance & no relatives to fall back on, so I don't see how very much could happen to us.

The worst is getting the kid back there. He'll be fine after we get there I know. And I think he won't even know he's making a trip. I'll be a little nervous about traveling with him, but when I get on to it, it will be swell.

Could it be at all possible for you to meet us in Chicago if we came on a week-end? If not, we can make it okay. I guess I can hardly wait to see you. We have to go from there down by day coach

How long does it take from Chicago? What town would we go to, Nashville? I wish we could live in Hoptown or Clarksville cause they are smaller, but I don't really care, I will live anywhere you can get us a place.

When should we come? You let me know when to come & we will. I'll ask Dr. about baby this afternoon & tell you what he says. Would be best if we knew that you were going to be there at least a month, but I will come when you say, regardless. By Oct. 1, he will be eating vegetables & maybe my milk would be all the extra he needs, & that would be swell because I wouldn't have to worry about his food. My milk is pretty strong.

PS —

In town — P. office. Baby on my knee. Dr. says perfectly ok. to travel. Will make reservations for bedroom soon as you say when. Write more tonite & Jr. weighs 13 lbs 7¾ — Love you,

Emy

It wasn't until November that the travel arrangements were finalized. We exchanged telegrams of our plans.

I had never traveled so far on my own, and it was a first trip for me alone with the baby. The agent at the Cheney Depot arranged a sleeping compartment for me. I had an upper and lower berth so the baby would have a bed of his own. Father gave me a hand full of silver dollars to tip the porters. Sunny proved to be a very good traveler, sleeping through the night. He charmed everyone in the car and loved all the attention.

On the train, I took him to the dining car with me, and he would gurgle and laugh and enjoyed seeing the people. He particularly liked a navy man, an older fellow with gray hair. He may have reminded Sunny of my father, because he went to him readily. The seaman wore lots of braid and gold buttons, but I never learned his rank. I would dress Sunny in his little rompers, and the seaman would reach out to hold him. He liked to trot Sunny on his knee, and he let him finger those shiny gold buttons.

One day he told me, "I like to hold the little tyke. He doesn't shed on my dress blues."

When the train pulled into the station in Chicago, Earl was there on the platform to meet us. Sunny went into his arms eagerly, which pleased Earl immensely. Earl had arranged for us to stay overnight in the Drake Hotel. The baby's buggy was checked through to Kentucky so Earl carried him around in his arms all day.

We had a grand time being tourists that day. Earl took us to see the sights of Chicago. We went to the Sears store and rode up and down on an escalator, the first one we had ever seen. We took a bus around Lake Shore Drive for a good look at Lake Michigan. When we went down to dinner at the Drake, we learned that Kay Kyser's band was playing. We had seen him play at Natatorium Park and loved his music. Because of the baby, we couldn't dance, but we enjoyed listening. Sunny clapped his little hands and babbled and cooed along with the music.

The next day we took the train to Hopkinsville, Kentucky. The soldiers all called it Hoptown. It was a pleasant town about the size of Cheney. Its streets were lined with beautiful old trees. Located in the southwest corner of Kentucky, it was about twelve miles from the border of Tennessee and ten miles north of Camp Campbell where Earl was stationed.

Earl had found us a nice apartment on the upper floor of a large southern mansion owned by a nice widow. We had a bedroom, a living room, a kitchenette, and a bathroom. An older daughter and her husband and two teenagers were also living in the house. A younger sister, whose husband owned a store in Louisville, visited on weekends. The busy household also included a deaf grandmother.

The family was interesting and very kind to us. The teenagers were pleasant and after school they often came up to play with the baby and to ask me for help with their homework. The oldest girl, Elizabeth, was in the seventh grade, and she wanted to give a talk about me to her class. She asked me many questions about our life "out west."

When she came home from school the next day, she had a list of things that the students in her class wanted to know about us. The west had been romanticized by Hollywood movies about cowboys and Indians. It seemed very far away to her, and she asked many questions. She said that it almost seemed that I had come from another country. Some days as I listened to her family, talking in their soft southern drawl, her world was a foreign country to me too.

The girls were sweet and very polite. They liked the baby, but never asked to hold him. I don't think they had ever been around a small child. And of course Sunny loved playing with them, waving his hands and feet and laughing with them.

The weather was warm like early fall back home. Skies were blue, and the trees were showing their autumn colors. Every day I took Sunny for an outing in his buggy. Sometimes we went to the store. It was on a shopping trip to the store that I learned about segregation for the first time. It had not occurred to me that such things still existed. One day I got in line to buy a few things at the grocery store. Immediately, a man came over and insisted that I change line.

"You are in the wrong place!" he told me. "You're in the darkie line."

It was only then that I noticed the door at the back of the store marked "Darkies." I was so shocked. I'm sure my mouth dropped open. I thought that such inequality had ended with the Civil War. That was how ignorant I was. I had never noticed any segregation in Seattle or even in the tiny village of Spangle. My father had always insisted that we treat everyone with respect. This was my first encounter with discrimination.

Sometimes in the evenings Earl would toss the baby over his shoulder and we would walk downtown to the movies. Sunny was a good baby and usually slept throughout the movie. After the show we stopped at the drugstore for a glass of lemonade. There were often other army families there, and we'd visit together.

We had our very first Christmas as a family in Hoptown. Christmas Eve we were invited to join the family downstairs for coconut cake and custard, a Christmas tradition in their household. We were lucky to have found such a lovely apartment furnished with old-fashioned chintzes and fine furniture. We felt at home with the friendly family and their kind southern hospitality.

A soldier could be in big trouble if he forgot his hat. So every morning at the sound of the five o'clock alarm, Earl would jump out of bed and comically clap on his hat. Then he would march around the room making faces and antics to make the baby laugh. Sunny loved watching silly Daddy and would clap his hands and giggle. I was always afraid that they would play so long that Earl would miss his bus.

We knew we were living on borrowed time. Earl explained carefully what we could expect. His unit could be put on alert at any time and sent overseas. When that happened he would not be allowed to come home and there was no way to let me know. So each morning we said goodbye as though it was the last time we would ever see each other. Despite the seriousness of the situation, we tried to keep our fears in the background and enjoy the time we had together. I asked Earl how I would know when he would leave.

"You'll know," he told me. "Though you will not be told, you will know. One of these nights, soon, I won't be allowed to leave the base. I won't be able to phone or send a message. Just some night I won't come home. That's when you must pack up quickly and go to bed early. You'll wake up in the morning, hearing the rumble of the trains and know we're pulling out. When that time comes, look out the window and you'll see our tanks on the train."

"Don't waste any time. Call a taxi and get to the train station as quick as you can. It will be really crowded getting out of here, since all of the wives will be leaving. So don't wait. Pack your stuff that night when I don't come home and be ready to pull out first thing the next morning."

"How will I know that you have really gone?" I asked, a hitch of tears in my voice.

"You will know," he told me. "The rumble of the train loaded with our tanks will tell you. Be ready to grab Sunny and go!"

Early morning rumble of train carrying tanks wakes Ernestine and Sunny. Earl is on his way to the war, January 23, 1945.

That is exactly the way it happened. One night a few days later, Earl did not come home. We waited supper, but it was no use. I had already packed most everything into my trunk, but that night I did as Earl told me. I packed everything except the things I needed for the baby that I would carry with me. I put those in my carry-on bag, and we went to bed early.

Sunny went to sleep quietly, but later in the night I began crying so hard that I woke him up. This frightened him, and he cried too until I took him to bed with me. I slept fitfully, waking often and checking the time, wondering how Earl was. I could imagine what he was feeling. I was so sad that I couldn't stop crying.

I must have drifted off to sleep. About 4:00 a.m. I was suddenly wide awake. The rumble of the train was not many blocks away. I ran to the window and looked out. There was no mistake. The long train loaded with tanks was going by. I could see it between the leafless January trees. I wondered where Earl was. I watched and waited to see if a passenger train came, but only the tanks kept rumbling by.

I realized that I had to get moving. Everything was ready. The baby was still sleeping. I ran downstairs to the hall to telephone for a cab. All the taxis were busy, there were none available. I should have known. Now what should I do? It was too far to push the baby in the buggy to the station.

Then I remembered. The man who stoked the furnace had a car. I ran down to the basement to find him. He said he would bring his car around and help me. By the time I had gathered up my things and got Sunny up and dressed, the man arrived and helped me take my things down to his car. The family was still asleep. I didn't wait to say goodbye.

When we got to the train station there was a bench full of army wives already ahead of me. Many had babies on their laps as I did. Older children hung onto their mothers. Everybody was friendly, but there was an air of tension as well. We all knew what was happening. Our men were going into battle. The 20th Tank Division had pulled out. The ladies from the Salvation Army were serving free coffee and donuts. We wives were heading home to wait. We all held back our tears.

It was a long, long day back up to Chicago. There were many delays as the train picked up members of a group of paratroopers heading into Chicago. There was no dining car on our train as it moved slowly north. We were crowded with paratroopers taking over the seats. I was lucky. The young paratroopers liked Sunny, and I always had someone near at hand to help me. One of them would jump off the train to bring me sandwiches from the little stands beside the depot when the train made a stop. I had milk in a bottle for Sunny, and he still nursed. But the only drink offered at the food stands was coffee. I didn't drink coffee so I got very thirsty. Finally a trooper brought me a paper cup full of lemonade.

It was an endless crawl into Chicago. It was dark when we pulled into the station. I had less than two hours to change stations and catch the Northern Pacific train going west. With the baby and all my things, I worried about making my train on time. As soon as the train pulled into the station, a young paratrooper stepped up beside me and opened his billfold, showing me a picture of his wife and a little boy.

"I have a family too," he said. "And I have to change stations here. Let me help you. Some soldier has helped my wife, and I'd be glad to help you."

Earl had told me that he and other soldiers always helped the wives with families get on and off the trains. I wasn't sure that I could manage to get there by myself. I was grateful for his help. As we lined up for a cab, one paratrooper after another would rush up and jump into the cab before I could get in. Time was ticking and I was getting worried. Finally the young man grabbed me by the arm, put his fingers to his mouth and let out a shrill whistle. Then he pushed a paratrooper aside.

"Stand back!" he shouted, as he shoved Sunny and me into the cab. "Make way for the lady!" Then he stepped back, saluted and was lost in the crowd. With the cab bulging with paratroopers, we arrived at the LaSalle Station and two soldiers took over. Picking up my things, they hurried us along the tracks and onto my train that was already loading passengers. They helped me to my compartment and stowed away my things. One soldier went to get me a coke and a sandwich. They sat with me and visited until the last call came. Then they rushed off the train and stood by my window, waving to me as we pulled out of the station.

We were going home. But where was Earl? I knew that he was headed for Europe. Soon after the train pulled out of the station, Sunny fell asleep. But I cried most of the night. I knew that somewhere Earl might be crying too. I don't remember much of the ride home. Sunny and I slept most of the time in our berth. Somewhere along the line I sent a telegram. Someone met us at the station in Cheney. I was so sad and I couldn't stop crying, and then Sunny would cry too. I couldn't stop thinking of sweet, gentle Earl going off to a war that he didn't want any part of.

On January 26, 1945, after I had arrived home, I received the telegram confirming that Earl and his outfit had shipped overseas. It said only what he was allowed to write. He was sailing overseas with the 20th Tank Division. It took much longer for his letter to reach me telling me that he had shipped out of Camp Miles Standish, from Boston to the European theater.

I knew that they were going to assist Patton's army in the final days of the Battle of the Bulge. The German army was desperate to hold on the territory and the fighting was fierce. Earl's time in the gunnery school had saved him from many deadly battles.

I did not hear from him again for several weeks when a letter arrived from 'somewhere in Holland'. I knew that Earl's position as gunner in the lead tank put him in deadly danger. His job was to set the big guns precisely on the target ahead.

Earl front row center with his tank crew, Camp Campbell, Kentucky

Home Front

It was a difficult time for me. I was numb and listless, worried sick about Earl. Safe at home with our baby, I read the papers filled with war news. I wrote daily letters to Earl, and he mailed them back to me with letters of his own. He wrote almost nothing of the battles he was in. The letters were all carefully censored. The winter dragged on. Snowstorms kept the roads difficult to drive. Cold nights brought howling winds. I wrote Earl every day but heard little from him.

Mother watched me fret and worry over Earl. The long days between his letters were excruciating. She knew I needed something to do. I had told her how much I enjoyed my train ride to Kentucky, so she suggested I take a trip to Oregon to visit Clare, who was living in Silverton, Oregon. Mother wrote my adopted sister Velma, who lived in Eugene, not far from Clare. This gave me the incentive to undertake another adventure.

I bundled up Sunny and again set off by train, this time to Portland where Clare met me and took me to her home. Clare's son was a year older than Sunny, and the boys had a fine time together. It was wonderful to see her again. We recalled the old times, and visited the historic towns in the area where she lived. We laughed at the diapers hung to dry over the fireplace, recalling our college days when we planned to have a famous Monet painting over the mantel when we set up housekeeping.

After five days with Clare, I went to visit Velma and her family in Eugene. Before I left Oregon, I also spent two weeks with my great aunt Ettie Blyue, my grandmother's older sister. She had been an early settler in the village of Crabtree in the Willamette Valley.

Now an elderly lady, Aunt Ettie was Father's favorite aunt. I met her only once when she came to visit my grandmother when I was spending a summer in Valleyford. Her voice was sweet and low, reminding me of my grandmother. She told me about the days of their childhood. She was 13 years old when her family crossed the plains to Oregon.

She told me of how she lost three of her young children all at once in a diphtheria epidemic. Somehow these stories seemed to jolt me out of my sorrow. I realized that we all must face our troubles and tragedies. So far I had been lucky. I resolved to be stronger.

It was already spring in the Willamette Valley, and with the soothing care of loved ones, I was able to recover some of my old cheerfulness. Anxious to learn if I had letters from Earl, I returned home to my parents. The snow was gone and spring was on its way. Sunny was happy to be back with his grandparents, and I was in a much better mood to carry on.

A few days after I returned, I received a letter from the Weyerhaeuser Company offering me a job. The company's insurance had covered the expense of the birth of our baby, and now they were offering me an opportunity to return to work. The company was building two housing projects in Spokane, one in the Whitworth district and one in Spokane Valley. They had rented an office in the northeast corner on the main floor of the Davenport Hotel and were offering me the position as secretary to the real estate agent who would sell the properties.

I enjoyed working for the company when we lived in Seattle, and I appreciated the insurance that covered Sunny's birth. I was happy to return to work for them. Edith, who had been working for Boeing in Seattle, returned home to help mother with the harvest crew and was there to help care for Sunny while I was at work. Sunny was now nine months old and beginning to toddle around.

I went to work on March 3, 1945, delighted to be back in the working world. The war appeared to be coming to a close, and airmen that had been stationed at Fairchild Base in Spokane were coming home preparing to continue their education, the Whitworth Project sold quickly. The Parkwater Project, in the valley farther out of town, was progressing more slowly.

As the weeks went by, Father became quite disgusted with me. He felt it unfair that I was off working and leaving my baby for my mother and sister to care for. Mother insisted that she didn't mind, but he continued to make a fuss over it. It was on the same day that President Franklin Roosevelt died that I reluctantly resigned from the Weyerhaeuser Company.

It was soon after that, on May 5, the day the war ended, that Earl wrote me the following letter:

VE day May 5,

The message "Cease Firing" came. That was good enough for us. A great feeling of relief came to us in our pup tents on the meadows of Salzburg at the foot of the Alps. The killing business is over. Some celebrated with a bottle of Schnapps, but most of us crawled into our tents and went to sleep with thoughts of home in our heads.

Slowly we put the role of soldier behind us there on the banks of the Chiemsee we started being kids again, learning to play again and put the war out of our minds, although the prospect of going to Japan was heavy on our minds.

Every day that we played we became more human. We lived like kings, with boats for fishing and sailing and water pleasures at our disposal. Recreation of all kinds was at our disposal. We were taken on tours to see Mad King Ludwig's castle and Hitler's Hideaway, a pile of rubble after the French got through with it. Trips were made into Paris and other towns to see the sights.

As beautiful as the country is, and the life leisurely, HOME is the magic word. And we were wild and happy when the orders finally came to board the trains and head for LaHarve and the boat ride home.

Love Earl

General Ward awards Bronze Stars, Salzburg, Austria 1945

War Buddies

During his years as a soldier in the 20th Tank Battalion, Earl's thoughts had never been far from home and the ranch. After the war ended, his last days in Europe were spent in the Army of Occupation, stationed near Salzburg at the edge of the Alps. They were not far from Hitler's mountain hideaway, the Berghof.

The liberation of Dachau was still vivid in Earl's mind. It was a day that none of the soldiers who entered the concentration camp would ever forget. There they had carefully lifted the emaciated bodies of victims who had been tossed naked into boxcars and left to die. The stench of the crematorium and gas chamber lingered, bombarding their thoughts when they awoke suddenly in the night. Struggling to forget the horrors of what they had seen, they did not want to talk about what happened there.

After the war ended, while his fellow soldiers spent their time playing cards in their tents, Earl wandered out into the alpine countryside. One day he watched a farmer and his wife harvest the hay that grew in a mountain meadow. Doing all the work by hand, they pitched the hay onto the tops of small trees, leaving it there to dry in the sun. The homey scene reminded him of the ranch back home, and for a moment the horrors of war were forgotten.

Out on the mountainside, the soft patter of summer rain sent the aroma of sweet grasses into the cool mountain air. It reminded Earl of all that he loved and missed at home. The desire to get back to the ranch burned inside him. His heart ached with love and longing for me and for our little boy whom he had only seen as a baby. He imagined the day when he could teach Sunny to throw a baseball or romp in the yard with Ole Baldy. His nerves were still stretched taut, attuned to the loud rumbling tank and the booming guns. He was still held captive by those memories. Only out in the fields, in the hills and valleys of the countryside, was he able to feel like himself again.

Earl resting in an alpine meadow near Salzburg, Austria

One day a fellow soldier, Fremont Stewart, went walking in the mountains where he came upon a brown cow grazing in a field. The sound of the bell that dangled from her neck attracted him. He wanted to take the bell home as a souvenir of the bucolic Austrian mountains.

Fremont had grown up in the city of Detroit and had absolutely no idea how to approach such a huge beast. He remembered that Earl was a farm boy so he must know something about cows. He went in search of him. Finding Earl resting in his tent, he talked Earl into going after the cow to liberate the bell.

Going back up the mountain, the two of them found the Jersey cow grazing in the flower-filled meadow. Earl's heart filled with sudden joy when he saw that sweet reminder of home. Fremont watched with amazement as Earl walked up, touched the gentle creature, and unfastened the bell from her neck. He patted the cow and spoke to her in a soft soothing voice. Fremont vowed to hang the bell in his home in Detroit as a reminder that gentleness and goodness still remained in the world.

Although they were opposites in upbringing and childhood experience, they found they had much in common. Both men had left a family behind, Fremont had a three year old son, Monty. He was a city boy who had gone to work for Ford Motor Company at the age of 14 to help support his family. Like Earl, he was no stranger to hard work.

The two young men first met in the aftermath of battle for the Munich airport. Earl was at his position as gunner in the lead tank in the first platoon as they went into battle. Fremont was the assistant driver in the third tank behind him. In the fierce fight to take over the airport, Fremont's tank had been destroyed.

Both men missed their wives and families and cared little for the drinking and carousing of the other soldiers following the end of the war. They enjoyed exploring the countryside together. As soldiers, they had done what was asked of them, but both were eager to return to civilian life.

Even after our taste of city life in Seattle, Earl knew he was a country boy through and through. His life on the farm had been centered around cattle ranching, sheep herding, haying and farm machinery. Through the long uncertain years of military life, his thoughts always returned to the ranch. He missed working beside his father, and the simple pleasures of country life. After army life, he longed for the freedom to make his own choices.

Earl dreamed of sharing his love of the land with his son, helping him to find satisfaction in the hard work and vigorous outdoor life of the ranch. In the quiet countryside, there was plenty of room for exploration. He wanted his children to grow up in the country as we had. He wanted the same comfortable relationship with his children that he'd had with his own father as they worked side by side. He wanted to go home.

Fremont Stewart second from right
Inspection Saturday Morning June 23, 1945 at Inzell Austria. "Our tank and equipment was rated superior. This was our new tank as we had lost the old one due to an 88.", Fremont Stewart.

My Soldier Comes Home

The first word of Earl's homecoming came in the newspaper. Lists were printed each day that told the names of the ships and the army units that were aboard. Each day we eagerly scanned the paper, looking for the names of the ships returning home with their precious cargo.

11,854 Troops Back from War

Armored units which smashed through Hitler's Reich were among the 11,854 veterans who returned yesterday on three transports.

The motorship John Ericsson, first to arrive, tied up at Pier 84, North River, with 7,562 soldiers.

The other incoming ships were the Sea Pike, which docked at Piermont with 2,761 troops and the Santa Paula with 1,531 soldiers, which docked at Pier 16, Staten Island.

The Edward Bellamy, with five casualties, is due today, also four transports bringing 3,029 troops.

Do your drinks get as *FLAT* as this?

Newspaper Articles August 1945

SOLDIERS ARRIVE FROM EUROPE

NEW YORK, Aug. 7.—Arriving here yesterday on the John Erickson from Europe were the following soldiers from the Inland Empire:

Washington.

Pvt. Charles E. Gruenewald, Leavenworth; Pfc. Roy E. Smith, Clarkston; Pfc. Wilburt Ferre, Toppenish; S/Sgt. Conrad J. Lauff, Cheney; Pfc. Sanford G. Bemiss, Clarkston; Pfc. James N. Brooks, Goldendale; Pfc. Neil P. English, Newman Lake; S/Sgt. Ervin C. Scheider, Yakima.

Pfc. Harry Koehler, N5203 Cannon, Spokane; Sgt. John O. Dell, Yakima; Cpl. John A. Runberg, route 9, Spokane; T/5 Harry J. Collins, route 1, Walla Walla; T/5 Ralph L. Morse, N125 Farr road, Opportunity; Cpl. Earl L. Hilton, Cheney; Pfc. Robert A. Coffey, Yakima.

T/4 Samuel J. Fazzari, route 1, Walla Walla; Capt. Robert L. Wilkinson, Colfax; M/Sgt. Robert P Steiner, Pateros; Sgt. Oscar Babb, Colfax; T/4 Harry Kin Walla Walla; T/4 Albert H. Ma tus, box 64, Lacrosse; Pfc. Willia R. Laughery, Wenatchee; T/5 Ar old W. Geiss, W1704 Riverside, Sp kane; Pfc. Elden D. Platt, Ellen burg.

209

What a joyful day it was when we picked up the Spokesman Review and saw the 20th Tank Division listed aboard the Liberty ship, the John Erickson, docking in New York City that very day. It was August 9, Earl's birthday, and he was coming home.

Our soldiers would have a thirty day furlough before they would be sent to the Pacific theater where the war was still going on. The great news was soon followed by a telegram from Earl that read "Meet me in Honeymoon Hotel." My heart skipped a beat. He was coming home at last.

Another Cheney man, Conrad Lauff, served in the same outfit and was coming home with Earl. His wife Bobbie and I quickly made plans to meet our soldiers in Seattle. Early the next day, I left Sunny with my parents and Bobbie and I took off for Seattle. As we topped Ryegrass Summit on Vantage Hill, the service station attendant ran out to the middle of the road, waving wildly for us to stop.

He was shouting, "The war is over, the war is over. The Japanese have surrendered!"

We pulled to the side of the road as the fellow came up to us and gave us the news that the war was over. We were as excited as he was, and after a brief but boisterous encounter, we got back in the car and proceeded on to Seattle.

This was such exciting news that we could hardly believe it. We decided to pull in at a little restaurant on the outskirts of Ellensburg to find a newspaper. As we stepped out of the car, a man came flying out the door, grabbed Bobbie and me around our waists and swung us around and around. He too was shouting that the war was over. It was former governor, Clarence Martin from our hometown of Cheney. We knew then that we could believe it.

We journeyed on to Seattle and checked in at the Moore Hotel where Earl and I had spent our brief first honeymoon in 1942. Tired from the drive over the mountains, we had just begun to relax when we had an unexpected phone call. Conrad's sister called to tell us that there was a bad wreck in Montana. A Great Northern troop train carrying soldiers back to Fort Lewis from New York had been rear-ended by another train and many soldiers from the 20th Tank Battalion had been killed. No names had been released.

Bobbie went to pieces. To lose her husband in a train accident after all the dangers he had braved in the war, had her unhinged. She became so hysterical that medical help was needed to calm her. For some reason, I was not so severely shaken. I felt sure that Earl was alive and well. I kept thinking about Earl's telegram. Although somewhat numbed by the shock, there was something that I was missing. Something didn't quite add up.

Suddenly it dawned on me. The telegram that Earl sent me was from Omaha, Nebraska. That meant that he was on a train on the Northern Pacific line. The troop train was on the Great Northern track, many miles to the north near the Canadian border. Earl could not be on the train involved in the wreck.

I called Cheney and the stationmaster at the depot confirmed that Earl's telegram came from Omaha. Our soldiers were not aboard the ill-fated train. Overjoyed at the good news, we settled down to wait. At four o'clock that afternoon, the door suddenly burst open, and we were in our soldiers' arms.

Outside on the streets, Seattle was going wild. The whole town was celebrating the end of the war. The four of us rushed downstairs and joined the crowds that were parading and shouting and throwing confetti. Strangers hugged strangers as the boisterous crowds filled the streets. At times the street was so crowded with people that it was impossible to move in the crush of bodies. Everyone was so happy, but none were happier than Earl and me, knowing that his fighting days were over.

We returned home a few days later. Sunny was happy to see me and clung to me joyfully. Mother said that he had looked everywhere for me, and kept asking for me. Earl brought him a little red toy truck that fascinated him, but he wasn't really sure about this strange fellow that had come into our lives. Did he remember his Daddy from those days last winter in Kentucky? Sunny kept close to me, eyeing his father from afar.

At bedtime each night of those lonely days, we kissed his Daddy's picture. He knew who his Daddy was and could point him out in any photograph. Sunny cautiously walked around Earl, eyeing him thoughtfully. Suddenly he ran into our bedroom and came back with his Daddy's picture that we kissed each night before going to bed. He had figured it out. He kissed the picture, then placed it in my lap and pointed to Earl, asking, "Daddy?"

I nodded yes, and he went to Earl, held up his arms to be picked up. Earl lifted him up on his lap. Sunny patted Earl's cheek, and looking at me with a big smile, he said, "Daddy" again. He had put it all together.

But it wasn't an easy transition. If my father was in the room Sunny would always turn to him first. When we would start to go out the door, Sunny would want to stay with Grandpa. It was the only home he knew, and it was only when he was older that he came to look to Earl as his father.

After a wonderful thirty day furlough at home, when Earl and his dad worked out the details of farming together, Earl had to return to Camp Cooke in Lompoc, California. Sunny and I went with him, and it was there that we learned to be a family again.

Ernestine, Conrad and Bobby Lauff in front of Moore Hotel, Seattle
Earl took this picture the morning after VJ Day, August 15, 1945.

Ernestine, Earl, Bobby and Conrad Lauff
Arriving home in Cheney after the war, August 1945

A Girl, a Baby, and a Motel Manager

Earl's furlough ended the first week of October, and Sunny and I went with him to Camp Cooke, California, near the little village of Lompoc. It was the mustering out post for the 20th Tank Division that had been on its way to Japan when the bomb was dropped on Hiroshima. Earl would spend the winter at Camp Cooke before retiring from the army.

The precious days of his furlough flew by, and when September ended, we packed a suitcase and headed to Camp Cooke. Earl had placed a piece of plywood over the back seat of our car, making a sort of playpen for Sunny, who played and napped in the car. We all enjoyed the trip. All went well until a broken water pump on the Ford stranded us for twenty-four hours in the little village of Shasta. This delay cost us money and also left us with barely enough time to report for duty at camp.

We arrived midmorning in Buellton, a stopover on busy Highway 10. Earl had to check into camp by noon that day. We found a small motel beside the road. Earl put my suitcase and Sunny's stroller inside. He handed me what money he had in his pocket, kissed Sunny and me goodbye and drove off, assuring me that he would be back to get us as soon as he could.

Sunny and I were tired from all the travel and were glad to be out of the car. We went to sleep early, but we were disturbed many times during the night by the noisy traffic. The next day we went out to enjoy the California sunshine. I took Sunny in his stroller on a walk out along the edge of the busy highway. He loved the cars swishing by, and especially

214

the big trucks. However, we soon tired of it and wandered off to explore the little roadside village. There was a big *Andersen's Pea Soup* restaurant in the hotel across the highway, but I knew I couldn't afford it.

Sunny and Ernestine

When we went back to the cabin, I purchased a loaf of bread and a jar of peanut butter, the manager at the counter asked me, "How long have you known that soldier that dropped you off here?"

I understood his concern. I'm sure the old fellow had seen many strange things happen in his roadside motel near the army camp.

"We grew up together," I told him with a sniff. "He's mustering out. He'll come as soon as he can. He will be back to get us."

Several days passed. We took our daily stroll and watched the cars swish by. I read Sunny stories and he took his naps. He ate his baby food and cereal. I ate my peanut butter sandwiches. I carefully counted the money Earl had given me.

I tried to stay away from the office to avoid the manager. The more the man eyed me, the more I worried. What would I do if Earl couldn't get back? As the days passed, I tried to ignore the questioning look on the manager's face. I was sure he had decided that I was just some wayward girl abandoned by a soldier who was never coming back. I figured that Earl probably would have to wait until the weekend to get a pass to leave the camp.

It seemed that as each day went by that manager got more and more suspicious. I knew Earl was coming back, but the nosey manager just shook his head. It was midmorning, near the end of the week, when the manager called to me.

"Hurry up!" he shouted at me from the door of his office. "You've got a phone call! It's that soldier who dropped you off. He wants to talk to you."

I was so glad to hear Earl's voice. "I have a three day pass," he said. "We'll find us a place to live."

Earl came at noon. He settled up with the nosey manager and helped us into the car. We drove down through a grove of eucalyptus trees that hung over the road, making a canopy of green over us on our way to the village of Lompoc. Known as the "Flower Capital of the World," fields of flowers were everywhere. Seeds from the beautiful flowers were harvested and shipped all over the world.

A few miles from camp we found a house for rent on a lettuce farm. It was a seed picker's shack. Tomato vines covered the sides of the porch. They were heavy with fat red tomatoes ready for eating. I fell in love with the place immediately especially after a steady diet of peanut butter sandwiches.

Earl came home every night. In the late afternoons, Sunny would watch for his Daddy's car to come down the row of flowers by the house. Sunny ran to the door and jumped into Earl's arms. Earl would hold him above his head and swing him onto his back and they would race outside and run up and down the lettuce rows.

We were told that we were welcome to take any vegetables left in the fields after the picking machines had finished. That was a fine treat. Some mornings the landlady would take Sunny and me with her to pick vegetables. We were in vegetable heaven, and happy to be together.

Postcard of flowers in Lompoc valley

Mustering Out at Camp Cooke

Near the end of November we were asked to leave our house in the lettuce fields. The owner's son was returning from the South Pacific and wanted to live there. Earl found a small apartment in Lompoc. The apartment was in a large house where a soldier lived with his wife, their little girl and a friendly dog. It was on the main floor, where we had a living room, one bedroom, and a shared bathroom. There was a tub for washing clothes on the porch, and a fenced yard with a big tree in the corner, a perfect place for little ones to play. We moved in just before Thanksgiving.

Earl's war buddy, Fremont, was sent to Camp Cooke with the rest of the 20th Armored Division. Fremont's wife, Edith, and little boy Monty had joined him. The Stewarts were living in a trailer park with no laundry facilities. Edith soon joined me on the porch where we washed out clothes while the little boys romped and played in the yard with the dog and their toys.

I was experiencing morning sickness and had gone into the hall bathroom when there was a knock on the door. I could hear Earl and Fremont talking. Fremont had come to get a recipe for stuffing the Thanksgiving turkey. He was doing the cooking because his wife Edith was having morning sickness. That was how we learned that Edith Stewart and I were both expecting. Our babies were due to arrive in the coming summer.

Earl and Fremont sometimes went out with a group of soldiers to the talc fields in the desert where they loaded sacks of talc onto the boxcars for shipment. This gave them some extra pay, and with money in our pockets we could leave camp on the weekend and drive into Los Angles to see the sights.

We loved the drive through the San Fernando Valley. It was a lovely valley dotted with the beautiful old homes of Spanish cattlemen tucked into the hillsides. Big gates with fancy ironwork showed the names of those old ranches. Sleek horses grazed on the hillsides and snorted and raced away from the fences when we drove by.

We often drove down the coast to Los Angeles. We watched for the big "Hollywood" sign on the hillside, drove past Forest Lawn Cemetery and into the heart of Hollywood. We would drive around to see the homes of Hollywood stars. We sometimes drove out to the beach at Newport or Malibu. Once we even drove to Del Mar in hopes of seeing Bing Crosby with his cronies along the fence at the Del Mar racetrack.

We had Christmas Eve dinner in the little village of Solvang and explored the old mission on the hill. We often drove under a canopy of eucalyptus trees up into the hills to get fresh water that flowed from artesian springs. On New Year's Eve 1945-46, we found a little hotel on the route of the Rose Parade in Pasadena and rented a room. The following day, we watched out the window as the Rose Parade went by. The theme of the parade was Victory, Unity, and Peace.

"THE QUEEN'S FLOAT"
Entered by the Tournament of Roses Association

Souvenir Postcard Tournament of Roses Parade Pasadena, CA. 1946

220 Green Meadow Girl

There was little for the soldiers to do at Camp Cooke as they bided their time. Their draft period lasted for the duration of the war plus six months. The soldiers had nothing to do as their final six months ran down, and they waited to be mustered out. Earl often ran errands for his sergeant and sometimes stopped by our apartment to play with Sunny and the dog during the day. One day he brought home a number of packages of socks.

"They're giving stuff away at the base. These are just what I need in my boots back home on the ranch," he said, tossing the olive drab wool socks onto the bed. "The Sarge says to take as many as we want. They'll just end up in some surplus store. I guess we're as entitled to have 'em as anybody."

As Camp Cooke was dismantled, Earl came home with work jackets, shirts and underwear, and even a new pair of boots. Since we didn't know how much money we would have once we were working on the ranch, every little bit helped.

Cheap gasoline was a fantastic treat after the rationing of the war years. We drove around the countryside as we used to do. We sang the old songs, laughing with joy when Sunny chimed in with his piping baby's voice. Being together was all we needed.

We spent our evenings talking about our future. Earl was enthusiastic about going back to the ranch. He made endless plans and wrote back and forth to his folks. Fremont and Edith sometimes came over in the evening, and the two men would talk long into the night about the futures they would build. Earl talked and talked about the ranch and how he was looking forward to being back home when spring arrived.

Earl and Sunny on porch at Lompoc apartment

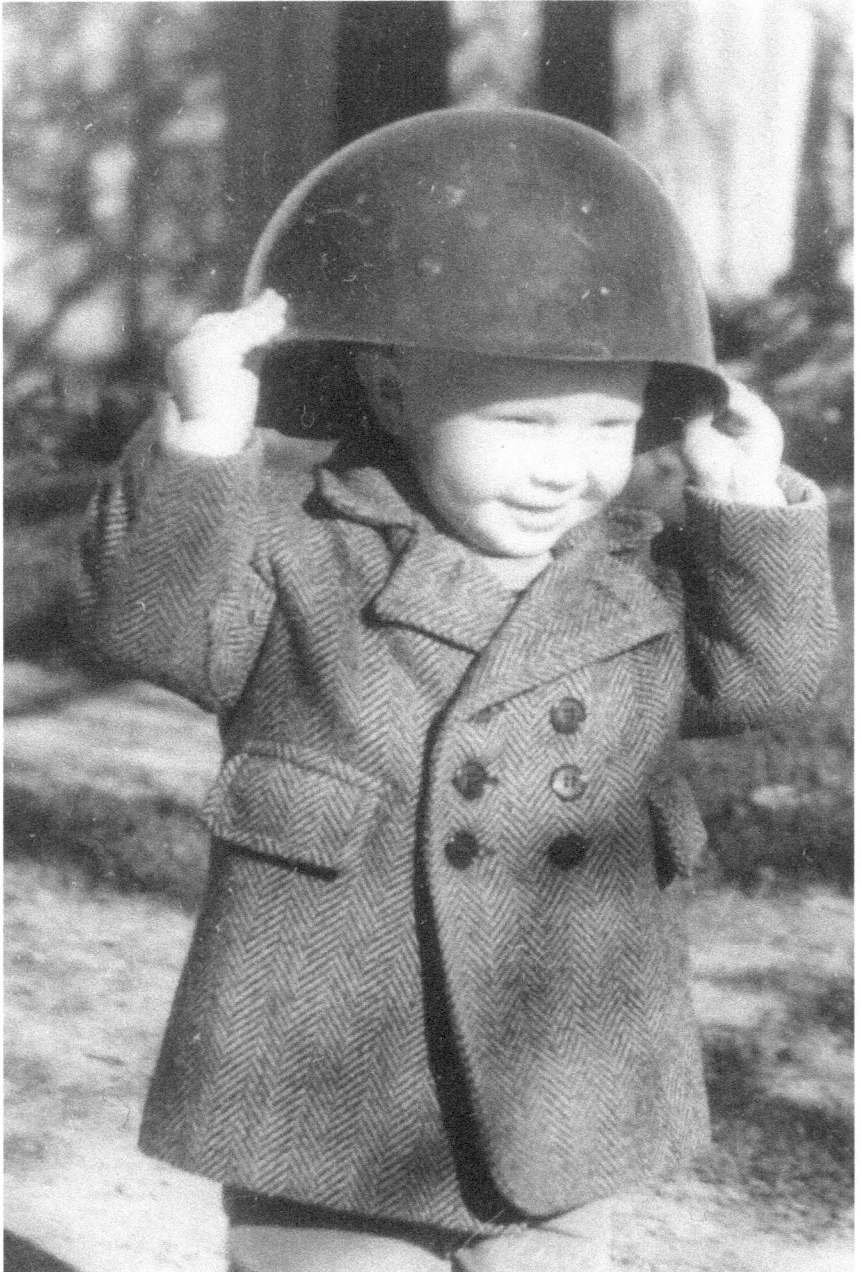

Earl gives Sunny his helmet

The Homecoming

It was a cold, gray March morning in 1946. Despite his eagerness, Earl guided our old Ford slowly down Depot Springs Road, savoring this moment of his arrival back home. A raw wind rustled the pine trees as we drove along the narrow country road, maneuvering slowly over the rutted ice and snow. Although the calendar read Spring, the countryside was still locked in winter snowdrifts so deep that we had been forced to wait in town until the milk truck came along to break a trail for us down the road to the ranch.

Less than a week had passed since Earl had mustered out of the Army in Camp Cooke, California. There near Los Angeles, spring had already arrived. Birdsong and the sweet perfume of mimosa and roses had filled the air. Green grass covered the rolling hills that surrounded the little village of Lompoc where Earl had spent the last six months in the army.

We had celebrated Washington's Birthday on the beach at Camp Cooke with Earl's army buddy, Fremont Stewart and his wife and 4 year-old son. The sun shone warmly that afternoon as we romped in the waves that gently lapped the sandy shore. Everyone was happy. The war was over, and we were going home.

Although we had scarcely talked of anything else, now we were silent with each other as the car skidded into the old road where the mailbox stood. Turning the car carefully down the snow covered lane that hugged the rocky edge of the hill, Earl rounded the bend at the bottom and dipped into a little hollow. There before us were the buildings of Rocky

Pine Ranch, spread out between the bluffs that defined the meadow's edge.

The sight of the old weathered house, the barn beyond with its sheep pasture and sheds was just as we remembered it, the way Earl had carried the memory in his heart all those months of battle overseas.

As the car plowed its way slowly through the drifts of snow that covered the road, we caught sight of Ole Baldy, Earl's sheep dog. There he sat, atop the little knoll where he had spent every evening since Earl had been gone, waiting for his master's return. As we coasted to a stop under the tall pine that stood between the house and the barn, the dog recognized the car and leapt to his feet, his tail wagging wildly, he ran to meet us.

Although Earl had been away a little more than five years, it seemed like an eternity. With tears in his eyes, he hugged me close as our little boy clung to both of us. The dog was leaping at the door of the car. Earl opened the door and lifted Sunny out and set him down beside Ole Baldy. Sunny threw his arms around the dog and buried his face in his fur.

"Well, here we are," Earl said quietly, as he watched the little boy and the dog. I opened the car door and Earl came around and helped me out into the snow.

"Here you are, married to a farmer," he said to me, looking at the old house on the rocky knoll. I was looking at the place my Grandpa had called the 'house with the sad face.' This was to be my home.

"We are going to have to live in the old house for awhile. The folk's new house is nearly finished. As soon as Dad and I get things straightened out here on the ranch, I plan to build us a nice new house."

"The meadow needs reseeding," he said, smiling at the little boy and the dog. "And I want to get started on my cattle breeding plan first, but I have some ideas."

He put his arm around me and I felt our unborn baby move. "We're home," he said. "We'll make a go of it."

His arm tightened around me. "What do you think?" he asked.

**Ernestine, Earl, and Sunny arrive home at Rocky Pine Ranch
March 1946**

I looked at the icicles, melting off the roof of the old house. There beside my foot was a tiny yellow buttercup, peeking out of the snow. Somewhere a bird called. I looked at the little gray brooder house, out under a tree, and I thought of my mother. I looked up at Earl's happy face.

"I think, that as soon as this snow melts, I will order us a hundred baby chicks!"

A snowy day at Rocky Pine Ranch

www.ingramcontent.com/pod-product-compliance
Lightning Source LLC
Chambersburg PA
CBHW030530100426
42813CB00001B/201